1000 SECRETS

Top Secret information from the most confidential
codes to the most brilliant disguises.
Invisible inks, hidden messages, technical data,
equipment, facts, spy signs, spy language
and inscrut̶a̶b̶l̶e̶ ̶s̶p̶y̶ humour!!!

Other books by GYLES BRANDRETH

JOKES! JOKES!! JOKES!!!
THE BIG BOOK OF OPTICAL ILLUSIONS
THE BIG BOOK OF MAGIC
THE DAFT DICTIONARY
THE CRAZY ENCYCLOPAEDIA
THE CRAZY WORD BOOK
CRAZY DAYS
THE CRAZY BOOK OF WORLD RECORDS
THE BIG BOOK OF SECRETS
CHALLENGE
SHADOW SHOWS
1000 RIDDLES: THE GREATEST BOOK OF RIDDLES EVER KNOWN
1000 JOKES: THE GREATEST JOKE BOOK EVER KNOWN
1000 FACTS: THE GREATEST FACT BOOK EVER
1000 QUESTIONS: THE GREATEST QUIZ BOOK EVER KNOWN

All published by CAROUSEL BOOKS

1000 SECRETS: THE GREATEST BOOK OF
SPYCRAFT EVER KNOWN

A CAROUSEL BOOK 0 552 54207 5

First published in Great Britain by Carousel Books

PRINTING HISTORY
Carousel edition published 1982

Text copyright © Gyles Brandreth 1982

Illustrations copyright © Transworld Publishers 1982

Carousel Books are published by
Transworld Publishers Ltd.,
Century House, 61–63 Uxbridge Road,
Ealing, London W5 5SA.

Made and printed by The Guernsey Press Co Ltd.,
Guernsey, Channel Islands.

1000 SECRETS
THE GREATEST BOOK OF SPYCRAFT EVER KNOWN

Gyles Brandreth
Illustrated by Peter Stevenson

CAROUSEL BOOKS
A DIVISION OF TRANSWORLD PUBLISHERS LTD.

INTRODUCTION

Did you know that an ordinary needle can be used to make a compass? That a lemon can be one of the most valuable pieces of equipment a spy can possess? Or that Julius Caesar had a secret code which agents still use to this day?

Well, these are secrets and in the world of espionage there are hundreds of secrets. If you are going to be a successful spy you will need to know these secrets to help you in your mission against the enemy. This book will help you.
All the information contained here is TOP SECRET so make sure that you keep it hidden, otherwise it will fall into enemy hands. Here you have 1000 secrets, from the most confidential codes to the most personal details about real spies. The secret ingredients of invisible ink, how to decipher secret codes, where to hide your spy equipment, how to disguise yourself to avoid being caught by an enemy agent, plus amazing facts and even secret jokes that you and your fellow spies can have a good laugh at. . . . . . . .in secret, of course!

All that you have to do is first look at the **secret key** and memorise the secret symbols. Then if you want a secret code you look through all the secrets with a pen beside them. If you want an invisible ink look for a bottle, and so on. It's quite simple really — but don't tell anyone, because that's secret!

SECRET KEY:-

CODES & CIPHERS —

 — SECRET MESSAGES

DISGUISES —

 — INVISIBLE INKS

TECHNICAL DATA —

 — STORIES OF REAL SPIES

SPY LANGUAGE —

 — SPY SIGNS

SPY HIDEOUTS —

 — SPY JOKES

FACTS —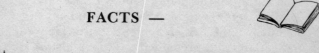

— SPY EQUIPMENT

A spy must be of 'average' build. If he is very
thin, or very tall, or very fat, he will stand out
in a crowd and be noticable. It is essential that
a spy can blend into the background and go
about his business unnoticed.

The author of the book *Robinson Crusoe*,
Daniel Defoe, was actually a spy and a
member of the British Secret Service. He went
to Scotland and pretended to write a history of
the area, but was in fact spying on the Scottish
political parties for the English government.

What sort of spy appears frequently at Christmas?

A min spy.

Secret messages written on a piece of paper can be hidden inside your shoe. If you think an enemy may search you then a **false shoe sole** can be made by drawing around your shoe, cutting it out and placing it inside your shoe. The message can be hidden underneath where no enemy would ever think of looking.

The yo-yo was originally a Filipino jungle weapon.

The colour used for danger in scientific laboratories is not red but **bright yellow**.

Two thousand years ago in Ancient Egypt secret agents had messages tattooed on their heads. Unfortunately, to read the message their heads had to be shaved!

A very useful **two-way radio** can be made
from two old tin cans and a length of string.
Make sure that the tin has no sharp edges —
it is important that a spy is in perfect health so
you must not cut yourself on a tin — empty
cocoa tins are best. Put a small hole in the
bottom of each can, thread the string through
and tie a knot. If each spy has a can and pulls
the string very tight it is possible for one spy
to speak into his can and be heard by the
other spy if he puts his ear to his can.

Fool the enemy by keeping your secret codes
written in a **code book**. This should be a copy
of any book, a book of Fairy Stories for
example, in which you have pasted blank
pages on which you write your codes. The
book can then be concealed in your
bookshelves.

A long time ago in England it used to be
much cheaper to send a newspaper through
the post than a letter, so people often used to
send newspapers and put pinpricks under
letters and words so that a message could be
read. Spies often put pinpricks under words in
newspapers today when they wish to pass on a
secret message.

If you sellotape or glue a small mirror into a
diary you can use it to look at what people
over your shoulder are doing whilst
pretending to look in your diary.

A simple but effective secret code is to write each word backwards. So, the message:

MEET BEHIND THE LIBRARY SHELVES

Would read:

TEEM DNIHEB EHT YRARBIL SEVLEHS.

A group of spies who work together are known as a **Spy Ring**.

9

All spies use various disguises to avoid being recognised by an enemy agent. The secret is to have as many disguises as possible and learn to change into them as quickly as you can.

A very effective invisible ink can be made from **lemon juice**. Simply squeeze out some of the juice and use it instead of ink. When it dries the paper will appear blank. To read the message simply warm the paper gently and the writing will appear brown.

A spy who carries messages or orders is called a **Courier**.

Clever spy signs can be made from **used matchsticks**. When left lying on the ground they can be split or bent to make small arrows and so point the way as a trail for members of your spy ring.

A **code** is usually made up of letters, words, signs, numbers or symbols. This means that a single word can represent a whole sentence.

A **cipher** is a system where every letter in the alphabet is substituted by another letter, number or symbol. When people refer to secret codes they usually mean a cipher.

To 'lift' fingerprints, dust the object they are on gently with talcum powder. Press a piece of sticky tape on to the print and carefully peel it off. If you then place the tape on a piece of black card you will be able to see the print very clearly.

 A great break through in modern technology was the invention of the **micro-dot**. A whole type-written page can be reduced to the size of a full-stop.

If you are in disguise be sure to avoid any dogs that you may know. They will recognise you immediately and rush over to greet you and give you away.

An easy but very effective method of passing messages is to take an old newspaper and **write your message in the blank squares of a crossword puzzle**. Write your message in the squares going downwards, filling in the words across with other meaningless words. No one will bother to even look at a crossword that appears to have been completed.

Whilst imprisoned, **Mary Queen of Scots** managed to receive secret messages that were sent to her. They arrived in barrels of ale in waterproof bags.

Can you decipher this?

TNEGA YMENE NA YB DELIART GNIEB ERA UOY

It reads: YOU ARE BEING TRAILED BY AN ENEMY AGENT.

What do you call a spy with very good manners?

You would say he is a-gent.

A **Double-Agent** is the name given to a double-crossing spy who happens to be working for two spy rings at the same time. He tells each spy ring the other's secrets.

12

To make your face look very pale pat some talcum powder over it.

In spy language if someone has the **'measles'** it means that they are dead.

 Vinegar makes an excellent invisible ink. Use it neat, do not dilute it with water. It will leave the paper blank when dry. The message will appear when heated.

A library can be a very good place for passing secret messages. When no one is looking, place your coded message on a piece of paper in the pages of a book. Make certain that you have previously arranged with your contact which book it will be (perhaps the end block of 'fiction', third shelf from the bottom, fourth book from the left). Once you have left the library your contact can come along and innocently take out the book.

When in disguise you must give yourself a false name.

 When you follow an enemy agent, or look for certain clues to help you discover his whereabouts, it is known as **tracking**.

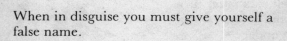

When writing with invisible ink don't send your message as a blank piece of paper, as this looks highly suspicious. Instead write an ordinary looking letter in ordinary ink, and write your message using invisible ink **between the lines**.

Most people can distinguish 10,000 different smells.

A hippo can run faster than a man.

There are times when a written or verbal message could be intercepted, in which case a spy uses a **silent signal**.

To make yourself look fatter tie a pillow around your middle with a piece of string under your clothes.

Someone who is disguised and is pretending to be another person is known as an **imposter**.

A pre-arranged place for delivering or picking up a message is known as a **dead letter box**.

People who devise secret codes and ciphers are called **cryptographers**.

Anyone who solves secret codes and ciphers is known as a **cryptanalyst**.

Believe it or not, a very good invisible ink is **onion juice**. The juice can either be squeezed out, or you can push a matchstick into an onion and write with the matchstick. The smell is sure to put the enemy off the scent!

A useful piece of equipment to have is a small piece of chalk. With it secret symbols and codes can be left on walls, lamp-posts, gravestones, etc. When your contact has received the message he can easily rub it out.

In the first century BC there lived a king called **Mithridates VI** who spied on the countries he wanted to control. He would go to a particular country in disguise, having learnt their language and dress. He was accepted by the people and was able to learn the weaknesses of the country and all that was necessary to take it over.

A secret code known as the **Bi-Rev** code looks very complicated, but is quite simple:

Take the message — **JOHN IS A DOUBLE AGENT**

Divide it up into groups of **2** — **JO HN IS AD OU BL EA GE NT**

Now write each pair backwards — **OJ NH SI DA UO LB AE EG TN**

And put it back together again — **OJNH SI D AUOLBA EEGTN**

Using the Bi-Rev code, try and decode the following message:

HTM ESAETS RYP SI OCIMGN OTINHGT

It reads: THE MASTER SPY IS COMING TONIGHT.

Milk can be used as an invisible ink if you use it undiluted. To read the message, warm the paper gently and the writing will appear brown.

When disguising yourself you can blot your eyebrows out by rubbing white soap on to them. Using an eyebrow pencil you can draw yourself new ones and so change your appearance.

If you think you are being followed (trailed) at any time go and pretend to look in a shop window. The glass will act as a mirror and you will be able to see if anyone is behind you.

One of the most famous ciphers is called the **Rail-Fence Cipher**. Take your message:

THE CODE WORD IS EDINBURGH

Now write it on two lines like this:

T E O E O D S D N U G
H C D W R I E I B R H

Finally divide the letters into groups of four. If your message does not divide equally by four then add a few extra letters on the end. These meaningless letters are known as '**nulls**'. So, your message will read:

TEOE ODSD NUGH CDWR IEIB RHXQ

Can you decipher this message. It is in Rail-Fence Cipher.

AEEY GNIT ALNM NNMA ETSR LIGE

It reads: AN ENEMY AGENT IS TRAILING ME

To make your eyes look older screw them up really tightly and draw thin lines along the creases to look like wrinkles.

A useful notice-board can be made for your headquarters out of polystyrene tiles. These can be attached to the wall and on to them you can pin notices, messages, and maps to communicate with your fellow spies. Do not put anything too secret on it though, just in case an enemy agent breaks into your headquarters.

A Kodak Matchbox Camera is a very tiny camera approximately the size of a matchbox, which can easily be concealed and yet takes very clear pictures which can be enlarged.

Thousands of years ago a Chinaman called Sun Tzu wrote a book on the art of spycraft which was published in 500 BC. One important quote from his book is something that any spy today should take note of:

"...what enables the wise sovereign and good general to strike and conquer and achieve things beyond the reach of ordinary men is foreknowledge."

What Sun Tzu means is that a good spy should find out about things before they actually happen. This means watching the enemy very closely so that you know exactly what his plans are.

A cipher, known as the **Gibb Cipher**, will
really fool the enemy. Simply replace each
letter of the alphabet with the letter that comes
after it. **A** becomes **B**, **B** becomes **C**, **C**
becomes **D**, and so on.

The word **ESPIONAGE**, for example,
becomes **FTQJPOBHF**, and **SPYCRAFT** is
TQZDSBGR. It's quite **FBTZ**, isn't it!
To decipher it you simply replace each letter
with the one **before** it in the alphabet.

Decipher this secret message:

**BO FOFNZ BHFOU JT DBSSZJOH
B DBNFSB**

It reads: AN ENEMY AGENT IS
CARRYING A CAMERA.

A meeting place between two spies of the same
spy ring is called a **RENDEZVOUS**.

A spy had to quickly hide a piece of paper
with a secret message on it and so put it in the
first place he could think of. He ended up with
a code in the nose.

One of the first people to use ciphers
extensively for secret communication was
Alexander the Great. It was in the days when
paper scrolls were used, but the message was
not on the paper, instead it was on the wooden
baton in the centre of the scroll.

A good hideout to eavesdrop on conversations
is in a cupboard or wardrobe. Position
yourself inside the cupboard before people
enter the room and then you will be able to
listen to all that they say.

The man who follows the enemy is known as
the **Shadow**. He will trail an enemy agent,
often for very long periods of time and
frequently in disguise so that he is never
spotted.

DOG

CAT

You can tell the difference between the tracks of a dog and cat quite simply: — a dog print will have claw marks, a cat's will not (cats draw their claws in when they walk).

A secret message can be written on a piece of paper using a **wax candle**. To read the message sprinkle powder or sand on to the paper — it will stick only to the wax and so allow you to read the message.

A quick method of giving yourself a moustache is to draw one on with an eyebrow pencil. It can easily be removed with any make-up remover.

A useful piece of equipment is your own thumb. Measure the distance from the first joint to the tip in centimetres and remember it. You can then use it as a measure.

Any information that is so secret that only a few chosen people know it is called **CLASSIFIED INFORMATION**.

To make yourself look different try changing the parting in your hair to the opposite side or even to the middle.

A fellow spy pulling on his left ear lobe means: **Meet me at headquarters at the usual time**.

One of the latest spy weapons is the BUW-2 ballistic weapons system. It looks like an ordinary gun, but can be fired under water. It can fire four missiles a second, so if you happen to find yourself chased by a crocodile he won't stand a chance.

If you are hiding in long grass, bushes or trees, then make yourself a hat covered in leaves, twigs, or grass to blend into your hideout. You will then be able to lift your head slightly to observe what is going on and remain hidden in the background.

If you unscrew a ball-point pen you will find there is room inside to conceal a piece of paper if you roll it up. Secret messages can then be carried and look just like an innocent pen.

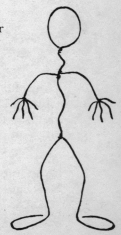

The letter which occurs most frequently in written English is the letter E.

An agent who specialises in electrical equipment and bugging devices is known as a **wireman**.

Add one teaspoonful of **honey** to a glass of warm water. Allow the mixture to cool and use as an invisible ink.

When writing with invisible ink it is usually best to write with a matchstick. Sharpen the end slightly by rubbing it against a brickwall or a piece of sandpaper.

A highly successful **compass** can be made using an ordinary sewing needle. Be careful not to prick yourself, the enemy could have dipped the needle into a deadly poison. All you have to do is rub the needle a few times against a magnet, always from the point to the eye of the needle, which will magnetise it. When you get lost simply hang the needle on to a piece of cotton and when it stops spinning the direction in which the eye is pointing will be north.

If you are not trailing an enemy agent the person you are following is known as your **Quarry**.

A miniature radio receiver or microphone that can pick up secret conversations in another room is called a **bug**.

What is black, has six legs, wears a disguise, and listens to people?

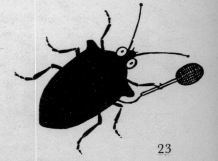

A secret bug.

A spy must be the master of disguise. Cheap make-up can be bought at any chemist. The essentials for any spy are: **Powder**, **rouge**, **eye-shadow**, **eyebrow pencil**, **lipstick**, and **cleansing cream** to remove it, of course. This is the make-up that women use, but a spy uses it in a totally different way to change his or her appearance.

Always carry a 'dummy' secret message about your person then, if you are caught by the enemy, you can keep the real message concealed and hand over the fake. A spy must never betray his own spy ring.

To give yourself a limp place a marble or small pebble in your shoe. This will make the limp look convincing and help you to limp with the same foot all the time.

Spies often talk in a language of their own called **DOUBLE TALK** or **DOUBLE SPEAK**. They have ordinary innocent sentences which have a totally different meaning to members of their own spy ring.

If you keep all your equipment neat and tidy and your headquarters clean and smart you will soon know if an enemy has been snooping around whilst you were out because you will notice if things have been moved or disturbed. If your headquarters are in a mess and very untidy you would never be able to tell if the place had been searched by the enemy.

In 1568 **Sir Francis Walsingham** founded the modern Secret Service as we know it today. He had spies in the court of King Philip of Spain and even in the Vatican keeping an eye on the Pope. Sir Francis was very successful and put a stop to plots to kill Queen Elizabeth I by Mary Queen of Scots.

Always carry a newspaper or comic with you when you go out, it could be useful to hide behind.

When you are out trailing your quarry and stop for a moment always keep in the shade or your shadow will give your presence away.

The very best spies always write to each other in a different code as this gives them practice in deciphering so that they can easily recognise a code when they see one.

To make your face look darker rub a little dry cocoa powder over it, but don't go out in the rain!

25

Secret messages can be concealed in a knot in your tie if you fold the paper up into a small square.

When spies meet and are given facts, information or instructions it is called a **BRIEFING**.

Julius Caesar invented a cipher which is still used to this day. In this cipher each letter of the alphabet is replaced by the letter that comes **three** places before it:

Alphabet:	A B C D E F G H I J K L M N O P Q R S T U V W X Y Z
Cipher:	X Y Z A B C D E F G H I J K L M N O P Q R S T U V W

By using this as a guide you can write your own secret messages.

Decipher this using the above method:

YFD U FP XOOFSFKD QLJLOOLT

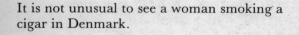
It reads: BIG X IS ARRIVING TOMORROW.

It is not unusual to see a woman smoking a cigar in Denmark.

When breaking a code, write it in very large letters with large spaces between the lines, then as you begin to crack the code you can write the message underneath the codewords.

A Hungarian wrote 32 lines of words on a single matchstick.

One of the most famous female spies of all time was **Mata Hari**. Her real name was Margaretha Zelle and she was an actress in Holland as well as a spy. Unfortunately she was very inefficient and many of the legends that surround her she made up herself. In 1917 during the First World War she was shot in France for espionage.

If leaving a sign put it at the side of a road or in the shadows where it will not be noticed or disturbed by anyone else.

Windmills in France and Belgium were used to send secret messages during the First World War.

If you find something on the ground, perhaps a notebook, diary or message, take a look at the ground underneath. If it is dry whilst the rest is damp, or if the grass is yellow at that spot, it means the object has been lying there for some time.

If you have a fringe or full head of hair try brushing it back after wetting it with water — it will change your appearance.

Any **fizzy drink**, such as pepsi-cola or lemonade, will make a good invisible ink. Write your message and allow it to dry — it will be invisible. To read the message warm the paper gently and the writing will appear brown.

A cipher which will confuse your enemy is the **Vowel Cipher**. The five vowels, as you will know, are **A E I O U**. When you write a message change the vowel to the next in the sequence, so that **A** becomes **E**, **E** becomes **I**, and so on.

The message: **USE YOUR EQUIPMENT AS ADVISED** will look like this: **ASI YUAR IQAOPMINT ES EDVOSID**.

Simple to decipher **when** you know the secret!

Decipher this secret message:

UAR CUAROIR HES BIIN EBENDUNID

It reads: OUR COURIER HAS BEEN ABANDONED.

28

Secret messages should always be written on **edible rice paper** so that if you are captured by the enemy you can eat it.

To read a message written in invisible ink hold the paper against a radiator or just above an electric lamp. NEVER use a match, and always take the greatest care not to burn yourself.

During the reign of Louis XV of France there was a very powerful spy called **Madame de Pompadour**. She developed a technique which is used even today in the government. This really is **TOP SECRET** — modern governments put wax seals on confidential documents, just as they did in the time of Louis XV, because to open and read the document you have to break the seal. So what Madame de Pompadour did was take an impression of the seal from which she could make exact copies of the original. She then broke the seal and read the confidential information. Later she replaced the seal with an identical one, made from her cast of the original. The document would then be sent to its destination apparently untouched because the seal was intact.

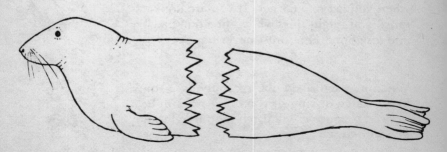

An effective burglar alarm can be made out of some old tin cans. Punch holes in the bottom of three or four cans. Thread some string through them and hang them behind your door. If someone opens the door carefully and hopes to creep in unnoticed he will find it impossible. As soon as the door is opened it will knock the cans and sound the alarm.

What do secret agents in an atomic plant eat?

Nuclear fission chips.

If you normally comb your hair back off your face try brushing it forward to give yourself a fringe.

When walking through a field or beside a river always walk on grass or leaves so that you do not leave any tracks.

Anything that a spy hides behind, whether a building, tree, or fence, is called a **COVER**.

When following your quarry take great care when you get to a corner. If you are not very quick you might miss which direction he goes and lose him. That must never happen.

When in disguise do not wear anything shiny, like a watch or ring, if you don't want to be noticed because it will catch the sunlight and give you away.

30

Binoculars are a very useful piece of equipment to have with you when you are out on a mission, but look highly suspicious. To avoid suspicion try disguising yourself as a bird-watcher.

A very lethal piece of technology is the invention of a Key-ring gun which, as it sounds looks, like an ordinary key-ring but fires poisoned arrows.

Many spies have a piece of equipment called a **Snake**. It looks like a thin tube and can be pushed through key-holes, into windows, or over walls and, by listening at one end of the tube, the spy can hear exactly what is being said on the other side.

To give yourself a black eye, brush some blue and grey eyeshadow around your eye and smudge it gently with your finger to make it look like a bruise.

31

Animals have a very acute sense of
smell, so if you are trailing an animal,
or if the enemy agent has a dog, be
quite certain to remain downwind.
If you do not the wind will blow
your scent towards him and the
spy will know that he is being
followed.

A good way of leaving a sign for a fellow agent
is to use ordinary leaves. Choose fairly large
leaves and put them in places where they will
not arouse suspicion, but where your contact
will see them.

A spy who specialises in photography is called
a **Peep**.

If you manage to get inside the enemy
premises a good hiding place is behind the
curtains at the window. If it is night the
curtains will be drawn and you can easily hide
behind them.

Apple juice can make a fairly effective invisible ink, but not as good as citrus fruits. There could be times when all that you have with you is an apple so make use of it. You can eat the apple and dispose of the evidence afterwards.

A pair of dark glasses will hide the upper part of your face. They also prevent people from seeing your eyes so that they do not know which direction you are looking.

When trying to decode a message try to discover which letters are the vowels. All words have vowels and if you see a word of one letter it usually means it is a vowel. Once you have established which are the vowels you will find it quite easy to crack the code. For example:

X LXKQ XCQ CRQZM

Now the first word is of one letter. Assume that **X** = **I** which would make the message look like this:

I LIKQ ICQ CRQZM

By looking at the message so far it now becomes obvious that **Q** = **E** which will give the message: **I LIKE ICE CREZM**. It is not difficult to work out what **Z** stands for!

If you are going to telephone a message to a contact let the telephone ring a couple of times, replace the receiver, and then dial again. This will give the contact a signal and he will know that it is you at the other end.

The clever spy changes his walk to match his disguise. Give yourself a stiff leg by tying a ruler behind one of your knees.

In America there is a special **SNOOPERSCOPE** which is very similar to an ordinary telescope, but has a special lens which enables the spy to see in the dark.

What do you call a spy in bed?

An undercover agent!

Bumping foreheads with a handshake is the traditional meeting in Tibet.

If you wear a different disguise every day this will really confuse any enemy agent who may be trailing you.

It is a known fact that for a spy it is more important to have brains than muscle. It is all very well being strong, but it is not always quite as simple as being able to fight your way out of a situation, instead you need usually to think. Just a little bit of thought can go a very long way.

One of the most tyrannical and evil men of all time was a Russian ruler **Ivan the Terrible**. He set up his own secret intelligence to search out any plots against his life, of which there were many. At this time there was a Russian proverb which says: *The walls have mice, the mice have ears*. We have shortened this today to 'Walls have ears'. During the rule of Ivan the Terrible thousands of people lost their lives because of the truth of this proverb.

Never walk along the sky line as everyone will see you, always keep in the shadows and out of sight.

A towel around your shoulders, under your clothes, will make your shoulders look very broad.

A rolled up tube of toothpaste makes an ingenious hiding place for any small object. Get a tube that is nearly empty and place the object along the bottom edge of the tube and carefully roll it up towards the top.

Never sign your real name if you are asked to put your signature on anything.

To take your fellow agents' fingerprints use their index finger. Roll the finger from left to right on the ink pad, pushing the finger down firmly at the same time. Immediately remove the finger and roll it again from the left side to the right side on a piece of paper and you should get a clear print. Take care not to smudge it.

Issue each member of your spy ring with an **identity card** with his photo, fingerprint, and codename. Each spy must show you his identity card at the start of each spy meeting.

A code that has been used for centuries is known as the **Sandwich code**, and you'll soon see why it is called that. The reason is because you make a sandwich with the letters. Take your message:

MEET ME BEHIND THE OLD BARN AT MIDNIGHT

Separate the letters:

MEET ME BEHIND THE OLD BARN AT MIDNIGHT.

Then sandwich some meaningless letters inbetween.

MBEFEHT MYED BGEAHLIPNFD TYHJE OPLWD BGAWRKN ADT MVIXDPNAIRGJHCT.

To decipher the message you just take out every other letter.

If you ever have to cross a patch of mud always walk backwards. This will leave a false trail and totally confuse the enemy.

Decipher the following secret message:

CFABNRCYEKL
THOMNGIDGWHMTSS
MLEREYTKIGNFG

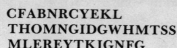

In the Second World War a well-known spy called **Christine Granville** cleverly managed to smuggle four pilots across the Yugoslav border by persuading the German soldiers that she was going on a picnic. They believed her!

If you have padded yourself to look like a fat person do not forget to rub some rouge on your cheeks. Fat people generally have nice rosy cheeks.

An umbrella can be used to hide secret documents and messages. Open the umbrella and attach the rolled paper around the shaft with an elastic band and close the umbrella up again. The paper is safely concealed.

A secret hiding place for small objects is a very large old book that nobody wants any more. Cut a large square hole in the centre of every page in the book. This will make the book hollow, although from the outside it will look like an ordinary book. Your most secret objects can be hidden inside the book and the book can be kept on your bookshelves. The more boring the book the less likely anyone is going to look inside.

Your voice can be disguised over the telephone by holding your nose while you speak.

A few teaspoonfuls of **sugar** in a tumbler of warm water makes a quick and easy to use invisible ink. The writing will appear brown once the paper is warmed.

Ainu girls of Japan often added a tattooed moustache to their upper lip for decoration.

One of the most famous codes of all time. It is made up of dots and dashes and is called the **Morse Code**. Each letter of the alphabet is replaced by a specific numbers of dots and dashes and can either be written, or tapped out (two quick taps for a dot and four for a dash), or it can be flashed with a torch in the dark, one flash for a dot and a longer beam for a dash. Here is the internationally used Morse Code:

A . —	J . — — —	S . . .
B — . . .	K — . —	T —
C — . — .	L . — . .	U . . —
D — . .	M — —	V . . . —
E .	N — .	W . — —
F . . — .	O — — —	X — . . —
G — — .	P . — — .	Y — . — —
H	Q — — . —	Z — — . .
I . .	R . — .	

? . . — — . .

Full Stop . — . — . —

Here is a secret message in Morse Code.
What does it say?

—— —. ·   ——— ——   ·—· ·   —·· ·   ———— ——·

·· ···

—·—· ·   ——— ——   —— ——   ·· ·   —· ·   —— —·

It reads: GORDON IS COMING.

Morse code can also be written as a series of
peaks, **low peaks for dots, high peaks for
dashes:**

A		H		O		V	
B		I		P		W	
C		J		Q		X	
D		K		R		Y	
E		L		S		Z	
F		M		T			
G		N		U			

Decipher this secret message:

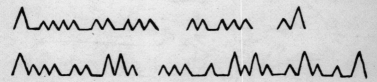

It reads: THIS IS A BIG SECRET

Did you hear about the Australian spy who made himself a new boomerang — and then went mad trying to throw the old one away.

An American spy called **Rose Greenhow** in the nineteenth century used to carry messages cleverly concealed about her person. Even if searched the messages were not discovered. Some were embroidered as a pattern on her clothes, others were in the soles of her shoes. Sometimes messages were sewn into tiny silk squares and were rolled into the curls of her hair. A lot can be learnt from Rose Greenhow's secret methods.

A spy must know the area in which he is operating like the back of his hand, so obtain a map of your local area and study the roads and landmarks very carefully.

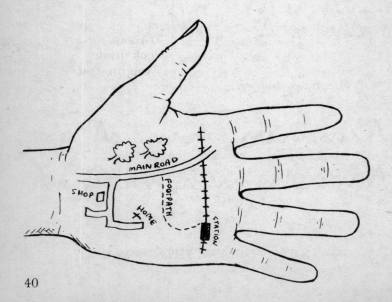

Small squares of black gummed paper stuck to your teeth will change your appearance and make it look as if you have some teeth missing.

Having searched the enemies headquarters it is essential that the room is returned to normal so that it looks exactly as the enemy left it and will never suspect that someone has been through the room. Returning the room to its original state is known as **DIRTYING**. If a room is left tidier than before the enemy is sure to suspect.

If you have to take a map anywhere with you, draw it on your handkerchief. If you are captured no enemy is going to look inside your handkerchief, especially if you pretend you have a cold!

The ingenious and successful spy will make a mental note of exactly what his room looks like every time he leaves it so that he can easily spot if anything has been removed when he returns.

Ties are usually hollow and are an excellent place in which to hide papers and messages. A safety pin will help keep them secure.

41

To disguise your voice try changing the accent. Speak in broken English, or pretend that you are foreign and cannot speak English at all.

Measure your hand span. Stretch out your hand as far it will go and measure the distance from the tip of your thumb to the tip of your little finger. Once you know the distance it will act as a useful measure.

When out on a secret mission it is always a good idea to take some food rations with you. Something easy to carry such as peanuts or dried fruit.

An invisible ink substitute can be a piece of **candle** or white wax crayon. Use it to write your message. To read the message rub over the paper with a wax crayon of a different colour and the writing will appear.

A very nasty looking cut can be made on your hand very simply indeed. Just spread a little Copydex on the back of your hand and as it dries pinch the skin together slightly to look like a cut. When it is dry take a red felt pen and draw a red line on the Copydex to look like a deep cut.

In 1966 a very tiny transmitter was invented by a dentist in America. It is called a **tooth transmitter** and is so can be fitted inside a tooth. It is controlled by putting pressure on the tooth. It is considered to be totally undetectable.

A spy who searches out
information is called a
Mole.

Always change your routine every day so that
the enemy cannot predict your movements.

A false pocket to your jacket can be a useful
hiding place for small objects. Take a square
of material just slightly smaller than the inside
your pocket. Sew around the three sides so
that it divides your pocket in half (leaving the
top open). You can now put objects in the
compartment nearest to you and pin it at the
top. You will now be able to use your
ordinary pocket as normal, and no one, even
if they put their hand inside, will notice the
false pocket.

If you are following bicycle tracks and come
across two and do not know which to follow,
the most recent will be the one that has cut
over the top of the other.

Keeping watch on an enemy, or an eye on
enemy headquarters, is known as
SURVEILLANCE.

Change your walk by taking very big strides. Place your hands behind your back and keep your head in the air as you go. This will make you look taller and give the impression that you are bigger than you really are.

Secret messages can be concealed in newspapers or comics. Write the message on a piece of paper and cellotape it to a page inside the paper. The paper can be left on a park bench or sticking out of a rubbish bin for your contact to pick up and read.

You can make yourself look bald by wearing a pink bathing cap. These are quite cheap, or your mother or sister may have one that you can borrow. To make yourself look partially bald stick cotton wool or crepe hair around it. Be careful not to use a glue that will melt wool or you might destroy the bathing cap. Copydex is good to use because it dries quickly and will peel off, so that you can use the same cap over again by sticking different colour hair to it.

A spy operating on enemy territory in disguise is known by the name of an **Undercover Agent**.

An unusual code is called the **Pig Pen Code**. No-one knows how it got its name, but it has nothing to do with pigs! With this code each letter of the alphabet is substituted with a symbol. If you are an observant spy, as you should be, you will realise that it is not a code at all but a cipher!

Decipher the following secret message:

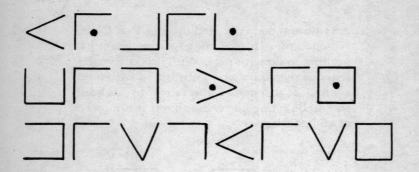

It reads: **TRAIL BIG X IN DISGUISE**

A highly secret government weapon is the **MBA micro-rocket**. It is only lethal at very close range, but is highly accurate. Some rockets are so small that they can be fired from an ordinary drinking straw like a poisonous dart.

Which famous spy was red, tasty, and delicious in a salad?

Tomata Hari.

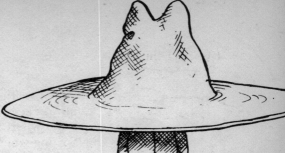

A hat with a wide brim can
be lowered to cover your
face and prevent you from
being recognised.

A pick-pocket who works for
an agent is known as a **Cannon**.

If you need a map of the area it can either be
embroidered as a pattern on a scarf, or if you
cannot sew then an ordinary piece of white
cloth can have the map drawn on it with
brightly coloured felt tip pens and worn as a
very colourful scarf.

Watch a dog or a cat walking and running
through some mud or soft ground and then
carefully examine the tracks. See how they
change when the animal was moving fast,
when they are deepest, and so on. This will
teach you a lot about tracking and what to
look for.

A strategically placed tree might enable you to
hide in the branches, concealed by the leaves,
and observe the enemy headquarters without
being seen. You might even be able to see into
a window if you are lucky.

When writing with invisible ink always keep your finger at the point where you finished writing when you need to dip into the ink, it will help you find your place again.

A useful way of sending codes is to use a dictionary, or any book will do as long as you and your contact have the **same** book. Go through the book and look for the first word of your message. For example, the word could be '**Have**' — this might be the **8th word** on **page 52**, so write down the page number followed by the word on the page. Now look for the next word of your message and write down the page number of that, until you have completed your message. A dictionary is a good book to use because it contains all the words you will need. A copy of *Alice in Wonderland* might pose problems if you want the words 'counter intelligence'!

A message using this code will look like this:

32.58 71.108 63.44 77.98 62.91 10.12

A long scarf can be worn around your head like a turban. Your face can be darkened with cocoa powder and you can pretend that you are from some exotic part of the world.

Morse code messages can be sent from a room with the light on by flicking the curtain up and down. A small flick for a dot and a longer one for a dash. If your contact is carefully positioned outside he will get the message.

If you have a pile of papers on your desk draw a thin pencil line down the edge of the pile. If the line is crooked on your return you will know that someone has been through your papers.

To tell if someone has been sitting on a chair, lying on a bed, and even how many layers of clothes they are wearing can now be detected with a new piece of technology called a **THERMAL DETECTOR** which reacts to warmth.

 Occasionally a spy is trained to be in a particular place long before he is actually needed. He is called a **Sleeper**. This is because he is put into position and then '**woken up**' when the time is right.

 Documents and messages can be taped on to the back of pictures and paintings hanging on the wall.

The tracks of a horse and cow are different. The cow's hoof is in two halves, whereas a horse's hoof is in one piece.

 You can disguise yourself as a vicar by wearing a smart suit. Cover your shirt front with a piece of black cloth tucked into your collar and a circle of white card as a 'dog collar' which can be fastened with a paper-clip at the back. A pair of glasses on the end of your nose and a Bible will make your disguise complete.

A good spy learns to use his eyes, moving them from side to side to see everything **without** moving his head.

In 1870 during the Franco-German War French agents walked out of Paris through the German lines disguised as priests.

Always try and walk on a hard road wherever possible so that you do not leave any tracks behind you.

In spy terms **SUGAR** is not something you put in your tea, but is a bribe. So never accept sugar if it is offered to you.

If you have a meeting in your spy ring always be certain to arrive on time. When holding meetings always hold them at different times, never hold a meeting every Thursday at 5.00pm as the enemy will soon get to know. If your meetings are on a different day every week nobody will be able to predict your movements.

An ordinary book can be turned into a useful piece of equipment in which to hide documents or identity cards. Simply glue two edges of two pages together to form a pocket, leaving the top open. Papers can then be slipped into this pocket and the book when closed can be put on your bookshelves.

The shape of your face can be changed by padding your cheeks with cotton wool.

You can occasionally help one of your fellow spies by causing a diversion whilst he goes about his business. If you pretend to faint, or lose your way, the enemy will concentrate on you and he will be able to study plans uninterrupted.

When you are tracking someone always look carefully at the ground for signs that someone has been there. Leaves that have been disturbed, footprints on the ground, broken twigs, etc.

What is brown, hairy and wears dark glasses.

A coconut in disguise.

Always vary your meeting places. Do not always hold meetings at your headquarters, meet at different hideouts, in parks, at school.

To completely fool the enemy two spies should dress in identical clothes so that they look exactly the same. Once the enemy has spotted you he will be certain to follow you in the hope that you will lead him back to your headquarters. When you are quite sure that he is following the two spies should then split up and go in completely opposite directions. The enemy agent will be so confused because he will not know which one to follow.

Search your headquarters carefully for loose floorboards. Underneath you might find a cavity. If it is small you can hide valuable documents and equipment underneath and cover the floorboard with a rug. You may find a large enough cavity for you and your fellow spies to hide in during an emergency.

With many secret codes and ciphers the words are split into groups of four letters so that each word looks the same and does not give the enemy any clue to its meaning. If the message will not divide equally into four then extra letters or numbers are added to make up the number, and confuse any enemy trying to break your code.

A secret message in Morse Code can be tapped out on a radiator or water pipes to someone in the next room.

An art gallery is always a good place for spies to meet for they can wander around casually pretending to look at paintings and pass on messages when no-one is looking.

When you have a meeting with members of your network be sure to have a good excuse as to where you are. Meetings should be arranged at times and places which will not arouse suspicion amongst your family. Never miss or be late for meals.

Half a teaspoonful of ordinary **household starch** in an egg-cup full of water can be used as an invisible ink.

If you are spying on a building that is being guarded, like a palace or government building, then choose a disguise that will not arouse suspicion — a road sweeper, a window cleaner, tourist, or dustman.

If trailing an enemy through the country look for signs, such as pieces of material from his clothes caught on barbed wire, which will give you a signal as to where he has been.

You must have heard of laser beams, but do you know what 'laser' stands for? It comes from the first letters of Light Amplification by Stimulated Emission of Radiation.

A code machine can be made using two discs of cardboard. One slightly smaller than the other. On the largest of the two write the letters of the alphabet in a clockwise direction and on the smaller one write them in an anti-clockwise direction. Put the two discs together, the smallest on top of the larger, and fasten them together with a paper fastener through the centre.

To send a message simply choose a letter of the alphabet, say **P** for example. Turn the letter **P** on the small wheel until it is against **A** on the big wheel. Spell out your message (keeping the wheel in this position) taking each letter in turn on the big wheel and writing down the corresponding letter on the small wheel. The wheel will give you 26 different codes, one for every letter of the alphabet. When you write the code put the letter **P** first so that your contact knows how to decipher the message.

Always have documents containing full details of all members of your spy network containing name and address, telephone number, date of birth, code name, height, weight, hair colouring, with a photograph and fingerprint of each one.

The head of any spy ring is known as the **Master Spy**. He controls everything that happens and sets all the assignments. Very few people ever get to meet him, know one ever knows who he really is, least of all his name. That is **secret**.

Wherever you are always try and wear the same kind of clothes as the local people, especially if you are in a foreign country, so that you do not stand out in a crowd.

If you ever use chemicals to make invisible inks, and you may have a chemistry set that contains the right chemicals for this, always treat each substance as if it were HIGHLY DANGEROUS. Never ever taste any of them and always wash your hands immediately you have finished using them.

When writing messages on edible rice paper be sure to use non toxic crayons and ink, for if you are ever in a position where you have to eat the message you do not want to poison yourself at the same time.

When you are trailing an enemy agent be sure to look back every now and again so that you will be able to find your way back and don't get lost.

Keep in your hideout a box marked **TOP SECRET** in which you keep anything that isn't secret.

Collect as many old clothes as you can to use as a disguise. Do not worry if they are too big, you can always pad them out.

'To test your tracking skills if you live in a town look out for any tracks made by birds on soft ground. Try and identify the tracks, or at least decide if the bird was a hopper, like a sparrow or crow, or a walker, such as a starling or pheasant.

In ancient Greece boys from the age of seven were trained for war and were taught spying techniques.

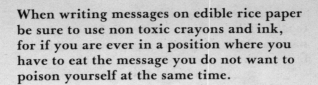

However clever modern technology may be, no one has yet invented a computer which can crack codes. Of course, computers can help, but it still needs a man's brain to help because the art of cracking codes really is a case of having a lot of patience and using trial and error.

Number ciphers are frequently used by spies. Simply take each letter of the alphabet and number them. There are two ciphers you can use.

Cipher 1

A	B	C	D	E	F	G	H	I	J	K	L
1	2	3	4	5	6	7	8	9	10	11	12
M	N	O	P	Q	R	S	T	U	V	W	X
13	14	15	16	17	18	19	20	21	22	23	24
Y	Z										
25	26										

Cipher 2

A	B	C	D	E	F	G	H	I	J	K	L
26	25	24	23	22	21	20	19	18	17	16	15
M	N	O	P	Q	R	S	T				
14	13	12	11	10	9	8	7				
U	V	W	X	Y	Z						
6	5	4	3	2	1						

To write the message use numbers in place of the letters.

Here is a secret message using one of the two number ciphers. What is the message and which of the two ciphers is being used?

7 19 18 8 14 22 8 8 26 20 22 18 8
4 9 18 7 7 22 13 18 13 24 18 11 19 22 9
7 4 12

It reads: THIS MESSAGE IS WRITTEN IN CIPHER TWO

If you need to take a map anywhere with you draw it on a very thin piece of silk and you will find that it can be screwed up into a very small ball and concealed about your person.

Ask grown ups if they have any old pairs of glasses that they do not want. If they have, carefully remove the lenses (they could damage your eyes if you were to look through them for too long) and if they are too big you will find that an elastic band or a piece of sticking plaster on the ends will stop them slipping. Glasses always change a person's appearance.

A cheap and safe chemical invisible ink can be made by adding one level teaspoon of **Copper Sulphate** to a glass of water. To read the message dip the paper in a solution of Sodium Carbonate (ordinary washing soda) and water, and the writing will appear blue.

 If out on a mission always take a pair of gloves with you and wear them if you have to touch anything. This will stop you leaving any fingerprints.

 Vases make useful hiding places for invisible inks and pens. They can also be used to conceal bugging devices if you want to listen in on enemy headquarters.

 Never let yourself be photographed under any circumstances. This will prevent the enemy from having a record of what you look like.

Secret messages and documents can be carried in a record cover belonging to an L.P. The message can be inside the cover and you can easily pass the cover to your contact saying: **'Thanks for lending me your record, I enjoyed listening to it.'**

Sodium Chloride (Common table salt) can be used as an invisible ink. Add one heaped teaspoon to a glass of warm water. Allow the salt to dissolve and the mixture to cool and it is ready for use.

With a few old clothes and some tools you can disguise yourself as an odd-job man and pretend to be repairing something outside the enemy headquarters. A large cap will partially cover your face too.

When using invisible inks, especially chemicals, always make up a new solution each time and destroy the old mixture as soon as you have completed the message.

Try and trick anyone who is trailing you into thinking that you are hiding somewhere. Go behind a bush and place your hat on top of a stick. The enemy will see the top of your hat just over the top of the bush and assume you are behind it. He will sit watching for hours whilst you make your escape unnoticed.

Messages in morse code can be sent in a park by tapping gently on the railings. If your contact is a bit further along the railings and listens carefully he will be able to hear the message.

If you think that someone is in disguise and might be wearing make up simply offer to wipe a smudge off their face using your handkerchief. You will soon see if it is a disguise.

A burglar alarm can be rigged up outside your headquarters with a piece of cotton and a tin can. Stretch a piece of cotton across the path. Attach one end to something solid, a stick pushed into the ground will suffice. To the other end attach the tin can and hide it in the undergrowth. When the enemy comes along his foot will catch on the cotton and the tin will clatter and warn you of his approach.

To make your mouth look thinner you can blot out your lips using a flesh coloured stick of make-up. Using a lipstick draw yourself some new lips of a different shape.

A cipher used frequently today is the **Typewriter Cipher**. If you have a typewriter then you can create your own cipher by substituting a symbol for each letter of the alphabet like this:

A	.	H	£	O	()	V	;
B	..	I	—	P	*	W	(-)
C	...	J	&	Q	?	X	'''
D	!	K	'	R	+	Y	÷
E	''	L	,	S	=	Z	***
F	/	M	(	T	%		
G	@	N	)	U	:		

A message would then look like this:

.. '' (-) . + ''   () /   & () £)

Which reads: BEWARE OF JOHN

Decipher this secret message:

. ; () — ! % £ '' * . + ' % () ! . ÷

It reads: AVOID THE PARK TODAY

Telephone tapping happens quite frequently in spy circles, it is a way of hearing other people's telephone conversations and gaining information.

When spies go out on a mission they use a cover name, such as Musgrave.T.Quinn, and they will use this name all the time that they are on the mission. If the spy has to sign anything he will sign as M.T.Quinn, not his real name.

When using invisible ink solutions be careful never to spill any and always keep them away from your eyes and mouth. Should any ever get near your eyes wash your eyes thoroughly with plenty of cold water.

A secret pocket in your coat is always useful. Undo a small stretch of the lining at the bottom. Stitch a small pocket from another old coat inside and pull the lining over it. Small secret objects can be kept hidden in this pocket.

When you write a message in code you **ENCODE** it. When you work out what a code means you **DECODE** it.

When leaving messages in places known as 'dead letter boxes', the dead letter box must be somewhere that your contact will normally visit. There would be no point in leaving a message under a table mat in an expensive restaurant if he only eats fish and chips, in a train if he travels by bus, at the cinema if he spends his free time at the football ground. The less suspicious the dead letter box the better.

A sling can act as a disguise. Not only will it make it look as if you are injured but it will also be a useful place to hide a small camera.

A cheap and safe chemical that can be used to make invisible ink is called **Ammonium Chloride**. Dilute it with just a little water and it will give you a strong and clear message.

A major break through was the invention of micro-copying. A very small piece of micro-film can contain enough information to fill a whole book. Rather than carry important documents around with him a spy can conceal a piece of film much more easily about his person.

When talking over the telephone disguise your voice by placing two fingers in your mouth.

 If you need to carry a small piece of equipment such as a gun or a camera but do not want it to be seen then all you have to do is make yourself a **false arm**. This can be done with an old pair of tights.

Take one leg of the tights and stuff it with newspaper until it is the same length and size as your arm. Stuff a glove with paper too and pin it to the end of the tights too. If you are really ingenius you can make it look really neat by finishing it off with a cardboard cuff. With the leg that is loose tie this false arm around your body and push the arm through the sleeve of your jacket. Put one real arm through the other sleeve, the other arm can be kept inside your jacket and can hold the equipment.

A secret message on a piece of paper can be successfully hidden inside a hat. Many hats have a small band inside which the message can be tucked behind.

Occasionally on a mission it may be necessary for you to copy a document, but you might not always have a camera with you. Do not despair. There is a very secret formula that will allow you to copy documents without a camera. This is how you make it:

One teaspoonful of washing-up liquid
One teaspoonful of turpentine
Two teaspoonfuls of water.

Using a sponge, brush or tissue, wipe this solution over the document you wish to copy. Press a piece of plain white paper on to the document and press really hard. Carefully lift off the piece of white paper and you will find a copy, in reverse, of the document. To read it all you have to do is hold it in front of a mirror. **The secret is to press very hard**. Rubbing the document with a spoon helps. Practice at first with a newspaper article until you become really experienced. You do not want to make a mistake on a mission.

A flesh coloured balloon cut in half and stretched over your head can give the appearance of being bald. The effect looks much better if you powder carefully around the edge to make it blend in with your skin.

To get information out of a captured spy casually drop some information that you do know, letting him think that you know everything anyway and he will tell you any secret you wish to know.

To fool the enemy jumble up letters at random to make it look like a real code. This is known as a SPOOF CODE. The enemy will spend hours trying to decipher it.

A daily newspaper can be used to successfully send messages to a contact. Take a pin and prick under a number on the date, say under an 8 for example. When the contact picks up the paper and sees the dot under the 8 he will realise that the message is on page 8. On that page you will have pricked holes under certain words to spell out your message. To read your message the contact has only to hold the page up to the light and he will see quite clearly which words have a pin-prick under them.

Philip II of Spain, who you may have heard of if you know anything about the Spanish Armada, is said to have used a cipher that contained over 500 different symbols.

Pretend that you have a bad back by bending slightly to one side and put one hand behind your hip. Walk very stiffly as if in pain. No one will suspect that someone as unfit as that is a spy.

If you are ever interrogated by the enemy only admit what they can prove and deny anything else.

Measure exactly how long your shoe is from heel to toe and write the measurement on the sole of your shoe. You will always be able to use it as a measure should the need arise.

Invent a special handshake that only members of your spy ring know about. If you ever meet and are both in disguise and unrecognisable you will know if you shake hands that you have a friend.

When you begin trailing a spy it is best to wear your normal everyday clothes to begin with. Carry your disguise in a carrier bag and you can make it look as if you are out shopping.

As people get older lines and wrinkles, which we call 'bags', appear under people's eyes. To make yourself look older you can draw in bags and lines under your eyes using an eyebrow pencil. If you smudge a little grey eyeshadow under your eyes too it will give a more realistic effect.

To improve your skill at code breaking try filling in a crossword puzzle, using a particular code.

It is most essential that a spy has a very good memory. If he has not and writes everything down it is possible that the written material could fall into an enemy's hands, even if written in code. But what is in your head only, nobody can steal.

One mental test to improve your memory is in the form of a card game. Spread a pack of cards out face downwards on the floor. Take turns at picking up two cards. **You must pick up two cards that are the same**, two aces, two twos, two kings, two queens, and so on. If you do pick up a pair then you keep them. If you do not pick up a pair you must lay them down again, which is where your memory will be tested for you could lay down a king of hearts, and two goes later pick up a king of clubs — if you can only remember where you laid the king of hearts you will have a pair! The one with the most cards when the whole pack has been picked up will be the spy with the best memory.

A chemical called **Bicarbonate of Soda** is used quite frequently in the home, for cooking, and sometimes for medical purposes too. You may have some in your own home. If so, mix it with just a little water and it can be used as an invisible ink. It is rather similar to washing soda.

To make an enemy agent talk when captured let him think that he has been betrayed by his own spy network. This will make him so angry that he will tell you all their secrets immediately.

Loosening your collar means 'mission accomplished'.

A destructable notebook is frequently carried by members of M15 and major spy networks. The pad looks just like an ordinary spiral bound note pad with a pencil. The pages, however, are covered with a special substance which makes them highly inflammable. To destroy the book the rubber on the top of the pencil is unscrewed which causes the pad to ignite and completely destroys it in around ten seconds. All that is left is a fine ash from which the enemy will be able to gain no information at all.

Using a red lipstick you can paint strange red spots on your face and arms to make it look as if you have the measles. No enemy agent will trail you for fear of catching something nasty.

To stop someone entering your hideout whilst you are away hang a sign on the door to stop them. **DANGER — RADIATION**, or **HIGHLY EXPLOSIVE CHEMICALS** should stop them.

A very good ink can be made from **Epsom Salts**. Just mix a little of the powder with some water. The only disadvantage of this ink is that it does require quite a strong heat for the message to appear, so it is not an ink to be recommended unless it is the only substance you have.

Furniture can always provide numerous hiding places for small objects.

Once you have received information and knowledge about enemy territory make a big map on thick card to use as a source of reference. Coloured pins can be pushed into it to plot the enemy's position, and similar markers can be pushed in to show where your own spies are situated.

Always put long clothes onto hangers when you are not wearing them, otherwise they will be crumpled and creased when you want to wear them and you will look highly suspicious.

To accuse someone of a crime of which he or she is innocent is called **FIXING** somebody, or giving them a **FIX**.

If you are crossing a stream try and use a bridge or stepping stones or else you will leave wet footprints behind you which the enemy can easily follow.

A special telephone called a **Cloak** is available. It looks like an ordinary telephone but can detect bugs, or if someone is listening in on a call, and will disconnect automatically.

A large old clock, especially a grandfather clock, will provide an excellent hiding place for any small piece of equipment. You will find that large mantle clocks have a small door in the back and often a hollow compartment at the bottom.

A small bug or transmitter is sometimes called a **SNEAKIE**.

If walking along a muddy river bank find two large leaves and walk on those, moving them into position each time you take a step. This way you will not leave any footprints.

Give each member of your spy ring a code name by which you can identify him. It is best to choose a theme so that perhaps the master spy will be **FOX**, his contact will be **RABBIT**, an agent will be **HARE**, a courier **BADGER**, and so on.

Here are some more groups of code names you might like to use:

THAMES	**BEETHOVEN**	**ROME**
AVON	**SCHUBERT**	**PARIS**
TRENT	**BACH**	**LONDON**
SEVERN	**STRAUSS**	**VENICE**
OUSE	**MOZART**	**MUNICH**
CLYDE	**BRAHMS**	**VIENNA**

To practice the art of disguise each member of your spy ring should disguise themselves as cleverly as they can in secret, they should then walk down a certain street (a busy street) at a pre-arranged time. Each spy must have a note pad and pencil and jot down any other spy he sees and what he is wearing. Later at headquarters you can all compare notes and see how many of your fellow spies you recognised.

If you find in a book a recipe for an invisible ink you will sometimes see the word **DEV**: written too, and this will tell you how to read the message — whether you have to heat the paper, brush it with a solution, etc.

Another name for a
Shadow is a **Tail**.

If shoes are too big
push some cotton
wool or newspaper
into the toes and
around the sides
to make them fit.

The invention of the **silicone chip** has
revolutionised transmitters because a silicone
chip is a mini electrical circuit that is invisible
to the naked eye. In fact 8,000 silicone chips
can fit into a thimble! That will give you some
idea how small they are. This means that any
equipment containing them can be small too
and easily hidden.

If you have been captured and want to send a
message but have no invisible ink then don't
give up hope. As a last resort you have a
useful substance in your mouth. Simply suck a
matchstick until it is wet and use your own
saliva to write with. To read the message your
contact can brush over the paper with a
diluted solution of blue ink and the writing
will appear dark blue.

An invaluable addition to any camera is that of a **zoom lens** which will enable you to take close-up pictures from a distance. They were originally developed for television and film cameras, but it was not long before spies began to realise their value and stole the secret.

Add half a teaspoonful of **Ammonium Chloride** and half a teaspoonful of **Copper Sulphate** to a glass of water and stir. The water will appear blue but will fade on the paper when it dries. To read the message warm the paper gently and yellow writing will appear.

An eye patch can be made by cutting out a piece of card the correct shape, paint it black, and attach a piece of elastic to it. It will make you look very different.

A code that will never be cracked if you are out shopping is the **shopping list code**. To an enemy agent you have in your hand an ordinary shopping list, but it is really a secret code.

A shopping list code could look like this:

Bananas	**7p**
Custard	**4p**
Oranges	**1p**
Kippers	**4p**

The list looks innocent enough, but the numbers by the side tell you that if you count that number of letters in each word you will get a message. The 7th letter of bananas is S, the 4th of custard is T, the 1st letter of oranges is O, and the 4th letter of kippers is P. Already we have the word **STOP** which is the beginning of a message. To practice this code make your own shopping list and finish what you think the message might be.

A clever piece of equipment is a hollow candle. Take an ordinary white wax candle. And cut off about three centimetres from the top and three centimetres from the bottom. Make a tube of white card to look like a candle and push the pieces of real candle into the top and bottom so that it looks like a complete candle. Only you will know of the secret compartment.

A hollow candle can be used to conceal bugs or hide secret documents.

If you sit with your finger touching the tip of your nose it will be a sign to your contact that you have a message for him.

The successful spy removes all the labels from the inside of clothes because if captured and searched these could give the enemy a clue to where he comes from. If all his clothes are made in Scotland, for example, it would be obvious that the agent has Scottish connections.

Always have a pair of soft-soled shoes so that you can trail an enemy agent without him hearing your footsteps.

A realistic moustache can be made by attaching wool or hair to a piece of sticking plaster. You can then stick the plaster in the correct position above your top lip and it will not fall off.

A secret message in Morse code can be tapped on a wall with a pencil or stick to someone in the next room.

The domino code is sometimes called the "**Rosicrucian Code**". It works like this:

A B C	D E F	G H I
J K L	M N O	P Q R
S T U	V W X	Y Z

You use a little grid like this. Each letter of the alphabet is indicated by the type of box in which it is enclosed and a dot to identify the particular letter being coded. So, **A** is ⌐ **B** is ⌐ **C** is ⌐ **N** is ⊡, **X** is ⌐, and so on.

Take the message:

RETURN TO HEADQUARTERS NOW

It would look like this:

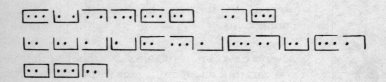

Decipher this secret message:

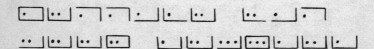

It reads: MESSAGE HAS BEEN DECODED

74

To listen to a conversation in the next room, if the walls are fairly thin, place an ordinary drinking glass against the wall and place your ear to the glass. You should be able to hear the conversation quite clearly.

If a secret meeting of the enemy is taking place in a bedroom, as is frequently the case, especially in hotel bedrooms, you can arrive before hand and hide yourself under the bed.

Russian and American spies often hide small pieces of equipment in bathrooms. A useful piece of equipment is a tin of talcum powder. Take off the bottom of a tin very carefully, you will find that it will come off quite easily (If not, then take off the top). Place the object inside the tin. Replace the top or bottom. Be certain not to place inside any object, such as a watch, which will be damaged or ruined if it gets powder inside it.

Decipher this secret message:

NFFU OFNSPE JO UIF QBSL BU GPVS P DMPDL

It reads: MEET NEMROD IN THE PARK AT FOUR O'CLOCK — each letter is replaced by the one that follows it in the alphabet.

If trousers or skirts that you are wearing are too long and will make you look conspicuous as you walk down the street try carefully cutting off the bottom and if you are not any good at sewing then glue them up.

A modern wrist camera looks exactly like a
wrist-watch. It has the advantages of being
very small, it takes clear pictures, and can
remain hidden under your cuff until needed.
When taking a picture it will appear to the
enemy that you are either checking your
watch or altering the time. As so many digital
watches today contain calculators, calendars,
and other equipment nobody takes any notice
if you are pressing buttons on your watch.

Practice your stalking skills by stalking up on
animals without them noticing. If you are able
to get quite close to a bird before it flies away
then you will know that you will be able to
follow close behind your quarry without being
spotted. A good place to practice is in the
country where you might be able to get some
good photographs of wildlife if you are careful.

Try and wear clothes that will blend in with
your surroundings and camouflage you.
Don't, for example, wear bright red in the
country — instead, if you wear a pleasant
green you will remain relatively unnoticed
amongst the undergrowth.

If you want to get information from a
captured agent then get a member of your spy
ring to act as a priest or member of the clergy
to whom the agent can talk to in 'confidence'.

You can remain hidden and yet see all that is
going on in the summer by hiding yourself on
the beach in summer. All you need are a pair
of swimming trunks and a pair of dark glasses.

It is essential to have several drops for secret messages. If you only have one dead-letter box and are being followed by an enemy agent it will be difficult for you to leave your message, but if you have several your contact will know, for example, that if the message is not in the hollow tree it might be under the litter bin at the bus stop or beside the pillar box, and he will know that you had difficulty leaving the message too. This will encourage him to be extra careful when picking up a message just in case he is spotted too.

Here is one of many alphabet ciphers:

Alphabet: A B C D E F G H I J K L M N O P Q R
                S T U V W X Y Z

Cipher: B D F H J L N P R T V X Z A C E G I
                K M O Q S U W Y

Take the message:

COLLECT SECRET PARCEL FROM THE AIRPORT

And it becomes:

FCXXJFM KJFIJM EBIFJX LICZ MPJ BRIECIM

   What does this secret message say?

TCPAK FCHJ ABZJ RK FBJKBI

It reads: JOHN'S CODE NAME IS CAESAR

77

An invaluable piece of equipment is a **dummy of yourself**. Stuff some of your old clothes with rags or newspaper. A balloon could be used as a 'head' on which can be put a hat or a wig. Once the dummy is completed it can be left in your bed if you have to go on a mission at night, just in case your bedroom is being watched. During the day it can guard your headquarters if left in a chair, with its back to the window, apparently reading a newspaper. Any spy looking in at the window would easily be fooled and would keep his eye on what he thinks is you, whilst you are out searching his headquarters!

A violin case or guitar case can be used to hide a whole host of items from tape recorders to volumes of secret books.

In some large departmental stores lifesize polystyrene wig heads can be purchased very cheaply. You could paint one to make it look like yourself and use it on a dummy.

A digital computer that can detect any stress in a person's voice is a piece of equipment called a **VOICE ANALYSER**. This piece of technology could also be called a 'lie detector' because you could easily detect with it whether or not an enemy agent was lying.

A plan to catch an enemy is known as a **SET UP**.

To disguise your voice on the telephone hold your mouth in a really big grin while you talk.

To fool any enemy who may be watching you from a distance when you want to pass on a secret message turn your head and look at something else or pretend to be doing something else at the same time, pretending that you and your contact are complete strangers.

Secret messages can be hidden on rice paper inside sandwiches. If a friend offers you a sandwich it is perfectly natural to have a look inside it to see if it is cheese or jam. No enemy will suspect anything if you look inside a sandwich before you eat it, he will not realise that you are reading a message.

Measure your own height from head to toe every three months. If you know exactly how high you are you can estimate how tall your quarry is.

During the First World War peasant women used to carry secret messages hidden in a basket of eggs. They looked so innocent that soldiers allowed them across the border, and even if they searched the basket they would find only an ordinary basket and eggs that were whole with no breaks or pin pricks in the shells. So where were the messages hidden? The messages were actually inside the eggs.

This amazing secret was discovered by German agents and you can learn the secret yourself. This is what you do: Obtain from your local chemist a powder called **Alum**. Mix a little of this with some vinegar and write your message using this substance on the egg shell. When the writing dries the message will disappear. All you have to do now is hard boil the egg and the message will go through the shell and amazingly appear on the white of the egg inside. To read the message you have to break the shell.

Your walk can be changed by turning your toes inwards towards each other as you go.

If two spies wear identical hats it is possible for a secret message to be passed. The agent tucks the message on a piece of paper inside his hat. The two can then visit a restaurant or library and hang their hats up. When they leave the building they can easily change hats without anyone realising. The contact will now have the hat with the message inside.

To find out if someone has used your notepad while you have been away place a piece of carbon paper two or three sheets down. If someone writes on the top sheet and takes it with him you will have a perfect copy of it.

If a contact across a crowded room places his index finger in his mouth it is a sign for you to **'follow him at a distance'**.

In the First World War secret agents used pigeons to send secret messages. They strapped a message to the pigeon's foot, although it was not always very reliable because sometimes a pigeon could take days to reach its destination, or never arrive. Some experiments were tried with miniature cameras that would take pictures as the pigeon flew over enemy territory, but again this was not very successful and the idea was eventually abandoned.

Beards and sideburns can be made by sticking crepe hair or wool on to sticking plaster. Sticking plaster makes a good base because it is flesh coloured, it will stick to you very firmly, and is also easy to remove which is important in case you have to make a quick change.

If you think someone is wearing a false beard pretend that you get something caught in it and attempt to pull it off. Don't forget to be very apologetic if it happens to be a real beard and you give someone's whiskers a tug — it could be painful!

Ordinary **tap water** can be used as an ink in an emergency. Write your message with it and allow the paper to dry completely. To develop the message brush over the paper with diluted ink (1 teaspoonful of ink to a small glass or eggcup full of water) the writing will appear in a darker colour of the ink than the rest of the paper.

Secret messages can be passed quite easily in a crowded discotheque. Wear clothes to look exactly like everybody else, dance only in dark corners away from flashing lights. You can dance very closely with your contact and as you occasionally brush past each other a message can be handed over without anyone seeing.

Bullet proof vests or body armour are important on dangerous missions. They are now made of a very light man-made fibre that is not heavy to wear, less than 2 kilos, and will protect you from most bullets.

A cipher that has been used for centuries is the **Inventory Cipher**. For this you simply make up an inventory, or list of items. In front of each item you place a number to tell your contact which letter of the word will give him the message.

An **Inventory Cipher** looks like this:

INVENTORY	MESSAGE
5 Trunks	5 Trun**K**s
2 Tents	2 T**E**nts
4 Covers	4 Cov**E**rs
1 Pillow	1 **P**illow
2 Basins	2 B**A**sins
1 Water Jug	1 **W**ater Jug
2 Lamps	2 L**A**mps
4 Trays	4 Tra**Y**s

KEEP AWAY

If you are on the trail of someone always use your ears as well as your eyes. Listen for the snapping of twigs or the rustle of leaves as he walks. He might also cough or sniff, even sneeze, which will tell you where he is. Good hearing is essential so that you can pick up the direction from which the sound is coming from.

Any instructions not written in code is known as a **CLEAR MESSAGE**.

What game do two secret agents like to play
on a train journey?

I-spy.

To disguise your voice try raising or lowering
the pitch.

When a contact gently strokes his right
eyebrow it means that there is **danger ahead**,
so proceed with great caution.

If you are spying on someone in a park on a
sunny day sit on a bench and pretend that you
are asleep. If your quarry comes too close for
you to carry on pretending, then hide behind
a newspaper. Two very small slits cut into
your paper will enable you to see through it
and continue watching your quarry.

To find out which direction the wind is blowing take a look at a dog. Before lying down a dog will turn around in circles to find which way the wind is blowing and faces it to scent danger.

The most popular of all ciphers are **alphabet ciphers**. Here is one that is used quite frequently. All that letters that use straight lines appear first followed by those that have curved lines:

Alphabet:	A B C D E F G H I J K L M N O P Q R S T U V W X Y Z
Cipher:	A E F H I K L M N T V W X Y Z B C D G J O P Q R S U

Take the message: **BRIAN IS A TRAITOR**

It will read: **EDNAY NG A JDANJZD**

Decipher this secret message:

LZ JZ BADNG NXXIHNAJIWS

It reads: GO TO PARIS IMMEDIATELY

Make sure that in your spy ring you have a **Cipher Clerk** — someone who is responsible for deciphering all your messages and who can write down all your codes and ciphers in a special secret code book. This is a very responsible job.

Most chemists sell a **styptic pencil**, which is a stick of alum which men often have to stop bleeding if they cut themselves shaving. You can use it to write a secret message. Warm the paper and the message will appear.

Disguise yourself as a newspaper seller by wearing an old raincoat, a scarf and cap, with a bundle of papers under your arm. If you are keeping a particular building under surveillance then you can stand opposite it in this disguise. If you are keeping a particular person under observation you can move from corner to corner in this disguise too.

If the building you are watching is in a town then disguise yourself as a tourist and stop outside the building to look at a map or guide book, or even load a film into your camera.

Stones can be used to mark with a special sign and left lying around for your contact to get the message.

To tell if someone has been looking through your things whilst you have been out you can do a little test. Leave a human hair lying on a pile of papers, across the opening of a drawer or window. If anyone comes in and opens the drawer or touches anything the hair will immediately fall off unnoticed, **but** when you return you will know that it has gone.

If you saw the following message you would soon realise that it is a code of some kind:

GARY EDMUNDS TOLD OLIVER UNDERWOOD THAT NIGEL ONCE WISHED

But can you see how to crack the code? It is easy when you know how. . . . . . .just take the first letter of each word and you can read the message: **GET OUT NOW**.

If a building you are watching is in the country disguise yourself as a hiker or rambler and stop outside the building to look at a map or take a stone out of your shoe.

A spy must be able to speak fluently in at least one foreign language. Not only because he may have to go abroad at any minute but also because if he is ever followed or captured by the enemy he can convince them that he is not English and cannot speak their language.

Why is a rich American spy very intelligent?

Because he has a lot of cents (sense).

Wigs are always good to disguise yourself completely. If you look around Oxfam and charity shops you can often find some that are quite cheap. Occasionally shops have old wigs from their shop dummies that they no longer need and are glad to give away. If you cannot, however, obtain a real wig then you can make one of your own.

Take an old swimming cap, hat, even half of a large flesh coloured balloon. Cover it with wool or string, either glue it on or sew it. Always start at the bottom and work your way to the top — that way the hair will overlap correctly and look neat.

If you want to look more realistic you can buy all different colours of crepe hair from a joke shop or theatrical costumier. Or if you happen to know someone who is a plumber you can perhaps get them to give you some binder string which looks just like blonde hair.

If the man you are trailing has a limp look for his footprints. One footprint (of his good leg) will be much deeper than the other. If he has a stick you will see the print of that as well.

Always be very suspicious of anyone who has their hand in their inside pocket searching for a pen. A new invention from Switzerland looks and writes just like a real ball-point pen but is actually a very lethal weapon that can fire a bullet up to a distance of 10 metres.

If a spy puts his finger
in his left ear it means
'Keep Away'.

If he puts his finger in
his right ear it means
'All is Well'.

What happened when the French spy jumped
off a bridge?

He went in Seine (insane).

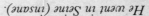

When sending a message in invisible ink, and
remember you should never send a blank
piece of paper, have somewhere on the paper
a symbol so that your contact knows how to
develop the message. An 'H' for 'heat', 'P'
for 'powder', and so on.

To spy inside your enemy headquarters one of
the best disguises to wear is that of a window
cleaner. You only need some old clothes, a
bucket of water and a cloth, and some steps. If
your fellow spies have done their job correctly
they will know exactly when the enemy is
holding their next meeting. At that time you
can innocently appear at the window and start
to clean it, hearing and seeing all they do and
say at the same time.

A very easy code to use involves a simple change in the way you write your message. No letters are changed or substituted at all. Instead of writing your message across, write it in two columns. Take the message:

FIONA IS COMING IN DISGUISE THIS AFTERNOON

and write it:

F	**G**
I	**U**
O	**I**
N	**S**
A	**E**
I	**T**
S	**H**
C	**I**
O	**S**
M	**A**
I	**F**
N	**T**
G	**E**
I	**R**
N	**N**
D	**O**
I	**O**
S	**N**

Take the letters row by row and place in groups of four:

FGIU OINS AEIT SHCI OSMA IFNT GEIR NNDO IOSN

Whenever you are trailing someone look out for landmarks, such as churches, garages, monuments, shops, trees, village greens, absolutely anything that you can memorise that will help you find your way back.

In cold weather you can tell if a house is completely empty because the windows will not frost over.

When is a spy like a bird of prey?

When he watches you like a hawk.

If a contact rests his chin on his hand it is a sign for you to '**return to headquarters at once**'.

You can detect if someone is in disguise by giving them a big hug when you meet. Whilst you are gripping them you will be able to feel whether or not they are padded, and if they have a gun on them.

When you are meeting a spy at a specific rendezvous point to pass on a secret message it is best to have a code name for your meeting point too. If you have 4 or 5 particular meeting points then number them or give them a letter A-E. All you have to say to a spy then is 'M-P.E' and he will know that he has to meet you at meeting point E. If an enemy agent happens to overhear you, or if he intercepts a written message with this in, he will not understand it. Even if he eventually works out what 'M-P.E' stands for he will not have a clue **where** it is.

Wherever you are going never take a direct route just in case you are being followed. It is better to set out early and take a long route and try to lose the person tailing you on the way.

If you ever visit an antique or junk shop you will often see little tags on objects. If you look at these tags you will see that they have a code written on them, not a price. This is because everything in the shop is a different price, and because there is no set price on an antique the shopkeeper can really charge what he wants. The secret code tells him what he paid for the object, so obviously he must not ask for anything less. If the customer looks rich he can ask for a much higher price than if the customer is obviously poor.

A secret message in Morse Code can be tapped out on the ground to a nearby contact with a stick. Or if the ground happens to be sandy or muddy then the message can be tapped out on a stone or tree trunk.

If you wish to use a code that will really confuse your enemy, however hard he searches in books, you can always develop one of your own.

If a secret agent was captured and abandoned in the desert why wouldn't he starve to death?

Because of all the sand which is there.

One way for a boy to disguise himself beyond recognition is to dress as a girl. A long wig can be made from wool or string, if a real wig cannot be obtained, and clothes can be obtained either from a charity shop or from a sister or friend. With the aid of a little make-up his appearance can be changed quite dramatically.

Up until a century or so ago there were still quite a lot of people who could not read and so to them every piece of paper even in ordinary writing seemed like a magical piece of paper. There is a true story of a boy many years ago who had to take a basket full of delicious cakes to a house about a kilometre from his home. Halfway there he felt hungry and stopped to eat one of the cakes, certain that just one would not be missed. But on arrival the lady of the house took a piece of paper from the basket, counted the cakes and then beat him for having eaten one. The boy thought that the paper was magic, and so on the following week when he had to deliver more cakes he thought that if this magic paper did not see him eat a cake he would be alright. So he hid the paper and ate a cake. He then replaced the paper and went on his way. Once again he was whipped for having eaten a cake! He did not know that this magic piece of paper simply told the lady how many cakes should be in the basket. The same thing could happen to a spy today if he had to do such an errand and the basket contained a piece of paper with a coded message. Which shows how important it is for a spy to master the art of code-breaking.

To discover if someone has been in your hideout whilst you have been out on a mission, place a very fine thread across the bottom of the door before you leave. If the thread is broken on your return you will know that someone has been in the room.

Why do Soviet agents always work fast?

Because they are rush'n.

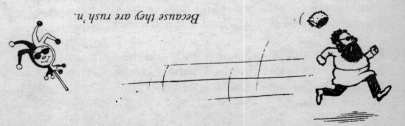

In twenty years of records, Thursday has proved to be the wettest day of the week, so do not make any plans for a Thursday which will be spoilt if it rains.

A chemical called **Cobalt Chloride** can be used to make a good ink. Mix it with a little water, about half a teaspoonful to one glass of water is sufficient. To read the message when dry warm the paper gently. Very occasionally once the message has been written the writing may stay pink on the page. This means that you need to dilute the ink with a little more water.

In the English language there are many words which are used more frequently than others. It is, therefore, useful to know which occur most frequently because one or two of the most used words will appear in almost every secret message. Here are the top thirty words, which should help you when deciphering messages:

FROM — AT — HAD — HER — OR — ARE — ON — HAVE — WHICH — YOU — NOT — BUT — BY — HIS — HE — BE — WAS — AS — WITH — I — IT — FOR — IS — IN — THAT — AND — TO — A — THE — OF.

If you are trailing a spy put any bulky objects in your back pockets and any flat objects in your front pockets. Then if you have to crawl along the ground you will find it much easier.

Anyone who teaches a spy his skills and the art of spycraft is known as a **Trainer**. Hence, anyone who is learning how to be a spy is called a **Trainee**.

What do you call a frog spy?

A croak and dagger agent

If you are going out trailing someone wear a coloured sweater and carry another one of a different colour in your bag. If you are spotted at any time you can quickly change sweaters and you will look completely different.

If you think that the enemy may have cracked one of your codes write a message and leave it at your usual drop. (If it disappears you will know that the enemy know where your drop is). In this spoof message say that you have a new drop, in a hollow tree for example. In a hollow tree place a fake message of jumbled up meaningless letters. If this message disappears too you will know that the enemy were able to read your first message and have cracked your code. Now that you know that you can drop that code and use another one. Also find a new secret drop in which to leave your messages.

A piece of equipment that will help you with communications is a secret code ring. All you need is a piece of wire, a bent paper clip, or even an old curtain ring. Anything that can be made in a ring and slipped over your finger. On to this ring place three or four coloured beads or tubes of card that you have coloured yourself. You must then develop your own code.

If, for example you place the red bead at the top (the other three will be on the other side of the ring and under your finger so not seen) it will mean '**danger**', a blue bead could mean '**you are being followed**', etc. You can also use combinations of beads so that red and blue together means something totally different. In this way you will get hundreds of combinations. You can even make the code more comprehensive by wearing it on different fingers. For example, on your little finger it could be all the danger messages, on your second finger it could be code names, and so on. You can do exactly the same thing with a code bracelet or necklace, but do not have more than six beads otherwise the codes will be too complicated and your contact could easily get the message wrong.

By using a dark eyeshadow you can age yourself by making shadows in the hollows of your face. Shade under your cheek bones where it is hollow, around your eyes in the hollows, and if you experiment in secret in front of a mirror you will soon find the best places to shade to make yourself look really old. When you have completed the shading dab your face all over with talcum powder to blend the shades in. Remember, however, that it is no good aging your face if you do not shade your hands as well (because they age too), and you must alter your walk and movements. Study old people in the street and see how they move and walk.

A cipher called the **Box Cipher** involves writing your message in a box. Draw a box with at least 25 squares and write your message with one letter in each square. You can write the message in a clockwise direction, anti-clockwise, from left to right, and you could also write the message in any code you wish, too, so that it is doubly difficult for the enemy to decipher.

Take your message:
THERE IS NO BOMB NOW

It can look like this:

Clockwise	ANTI clockwise	Left to right
T H E R	B O N S	T H E R
MB N E	O WO I	E I S N
O WO I	MB N E	O B O M
B O N S	T H E R	B NO W

Decipher this secret message:

I O D U
A T I I
M I S S
N N G E

ƃspɹɐʍuʍop pɐǝɹ sı ǝƃɐssǝɯ ǝɥ┴
Ⴝᔕ∩פᴚ∩∀ ∩Ⴝ ┴ON W∀ I :sⅼⱯㄣ┴

Good powers of observation are essential to a spy. When you have some free time with nothing to do, take a note book and go and sit in some public place and watch people.

What does a good spy have between his eyes?

Something that smells.

If the enemy you are trailing is in a car then a
very good disguise to wear is that of a motor-
cyclist. The crash helmet and goggles will
disguise your face, as will a leather jacket and
gloves. With a motor cycle you will be able,
only if you are a skilled rider, to follow the car
at quite close range.

When in disguise a spy will have a wallet with
him that contains items connected with the
person he is meant to be. Inside there will be
letters addressed to him under his false name.
There will be a false driving licence, a false
diary filled with false information, stamps and
coins from the country he says he comes from,
fake photographs of his family. If he is
captured his wallet is sure to be searched and
the evidence inside will back up his story.

If a spy stands with his arms folded and
whistles the National Anthem it is a sign for
you to '**meet him at the hideout
immediately**'.

Devise a secret knock as a code that your spies
can tap on the door when they are outside. If
you hear this secret knock you will know that
it is a member of your spy ring outside and
you can safely let them in. If you hear a
strange knock you will know that it is an
enemy outside and the door should only be
opened with very great care.

Grapefruit juice can be squeezed out very easily from the fruit and used as an ink. Develop the message by heating the paper. If a spy has a grapefruit for breakfast he can write the message then, pretending that he or she is writing a shopping list or merely jotting down things that have to be done that day. That way no one will suspect anything. If you get up early and have your breakfast any enemy agents will still be in bed and so will not see what you are doing.

The passing of information from an agent to a courier in apparently everyday activities, such as whilst shopping in the supermarket (the swapping of baskets), while playing football, or at the cinema is known as **BRUSH CONTACT**.

Rather than writing a whole message in invisible ink an ordinary and innocent looking letter can be written with particular words underlined or circled in invisible ink to spell out the message. When the spy receives the letter he has only to heat the paper and the ringed words will appear and give him the message.

If you think a woman may be a man in disguise then try and frighten 'her' in some way. If she screams and runs away you will be able to tell by the way she runs whether or not it is a man.

To listen to a conversation in a restaurant hide under a table if it has a very long cloth so that you are completely concealed.

 What happened to the agent who took a train home?

The Master Spy made him take it back.

If you think an egg may be hard boiled and contains a message (by the method described earlier) try spinning the egg. Only hard boiled eggs will spin.

To make your hair appear grey dab a little talcum powder or flour on to it. It should brush out quite easily afterwards. Take care not to go out in the rain, otherwise your hair will return to its normal colour and everyone will see through your disguise.

 If you capture an enemy agent you can get him to tell you all his secrets by threatening him with the Truth Drug. The greatest secret of all, however, is the ingredients for the Truth Drug which **nobody** knows yet.

A code that has been in use for over three hundred years is known as **Trevanion's Code**, name after one of King Charles' cavaliers imprisoned in Colchester Castle during the English Civil War. It is quite simple to use but very effective. All you have to do is send a quite innocent looking letter. To read your message your contact will take out every third word following a punctuation mark. This simple message:

Dear Ian,

> *We will leave our dog at your house this week, and come after him again later in the week. Probably at midnight owing to the late arrival of our train.*

> *See you tomorrow,*
> *Tony.*

Gives you the secret message: **LEAVE AFTER MIDNIGHT TOMORROW.**

 A message in Morse Code can be flashed from a window by covering the bulb on a table lamp with your hat.

When stalking your quarry never have anything hanging around your neck, such as a camera or binoculars. Not only will they slow you down, but they could very easily get caught on a tree or branch as you go along.

Attempting to discover another country's plans and how their spy rings operate is known as **COUNTER ESPIONAGE**.

When do secret agents work in shops?

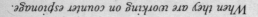

When they are working on counter espionage.

To see if someone has been in your headquarters whilst you have been out open your
drawer very slightly before you go and draw a
thin pencil line on the side or underneath the
drawer to mark its position. If the line has
moved on your return you will know that
someone has been through your things.

Matchsticks can be used to send secret
messages. You can put a message in Morse
Code in dots and dashes on the side of a used
match and leave it lying in a strategic
position.

If a spy taps the right hand side of his nose
gently with his index finger it means that he
has some secret information for you.

You can make your nose appear longer and
thin by using some dark eye shadow to shade
the sides of your nose.

A courier in a spy ring is sometimes known as
the **POSTMAN** because he is the one that
delivers secret messages.

A unique cipher is called the **Double-Dutch Cipher** and you can use the basic principle of it to develop your own cipher. All you have to do is choose a syllable, such as **IP** and add it after every consonant in your word.

Infra-red film has invisible rays that can film things not normally visible to the naked eye, so is used quite frequently by spies. It has the added advantage of being able to film through mist. So if you are out on a foggy day you can still film a clear picture of the surroundings.

If it is a cold winters day you can skillfully disguise yourself by wearing thick clothes (to disguise your figure) and wearing a woolly hat to cover your hair and a long scarf which can go over your mouth and nose. No one will take any notice of you because lots of people dress like that on a cold day anyway.

Secret messages can be left lying around in the form of knots on a piece of string. An ordinary loop knot can make the equivalent of a dot and a knot in the figure-of-eight manner will give you the equivalent of a dash. A whole message in Morse Code can be put on a piece of string in this way.

Morse code messages knotted on to a piece of string have an added advantage in that an agent can feel the knots with his hands and so 'read' the message in the dark.

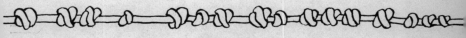

An English sentence that contains all the letters of the alphabet is "**Jackdaws love my big sphinx of quartz**". It can be used to test your knowledge of secret codes, because to write it in code you will need to know every symbol, letter or number.

A variation of the Double Dutch Cipher is to take whatever syllable you choose (say **IP**, for example) and place it in front of every vowel in your message. The word **ESPIONAGE** would become **IPESPIPIIPONIPAGEIPE**! The word **DISGUISE** becomes **DIPISGIPUIPISIPE**. You can use any syllable you wish.

Can you decipher this secret message using the above cipher?

CLINAINUDINE INIS INOINUT INOF GINAINOL INAGINAININ

It reads: CLAUDE IS OUT OF GAOL AGAIN.

How could the spy tell the weather with a piece of string?

If it moved about it was windy, if it was wet it was raining.

If you are being watched by an enemy you are said to be **ILL**.

If you see a piece of string hanging over a branch in the form of a noose it means that there is danger ahead.

Before leaving your headquarters make sure that all your pencils and crayons have a very sharp point. You will soon be able to tell if someone has used one when you return because it will not be sharp.

A message can sometimes be placed in a 'moving drop' such as a train or a bus. This has the advantage that the courier and his contact can be kilometres apart before the message is received. The courier can get off the bus or train at the stop **before** the contact gets on, just as long as the pick up place for the message has been pre-arranged.

There are many number ciphers, as we have already seen, but you do not have to use the numbers 1 – 26 just because there are 26 letters in the alphabet. You can use absolutely any numbers you wish, like this:

A	B	C	D	E	F	G	H	I	J	K
297	298	299	300	301	302	303	304	305	306	307

L	M	N	O	P	Q	R	S	T	U	V
308	309	310	311	312	313	314	315	316	317	318

W	X	Y	Z
319	320	321	322

The message: **LOOK OUT** would read:
308 311 311 307 311 317 316

Unless the enemy actually knew the cipher it would be incredibly difficult to work out.

What four letters does a spy use when he spots an enemy agent?

U-C-I-O.

It is quite useful to have a special symbol for
your own spy ring, a symbol which can
appear on your note-paper, your own secret
documents, your spies' identity cards and so
on. The simplest method is to use a stamp of
some kind.

 A stamp can be made by cutting a potato in
half and carefully cutting out a design,
perhaps a skull and crossbones, or a small
symbol of your own, even your own initials.
Once you have cut it you can press it on to an
ink pad and print it on to any paper you wish.
This will give all your papers a special identification mark which will be impossible for
the enemy to forge.

It is now possible to buy very small amplifiers,
smaller than a cigarette packet, which are so
powerful that they can pick up the sound of a
wristwatch ticking up to 15 metres away. A
very useful piece of equipment for picking up
conversations in another room or the voices of
two people further down a corridor.

A cipher that was used in the time of Julius Caesar is a simple **Roman cipher**, using the number code system, but substituting letters of the alphabet with Roman Numerals:

A	B	C	D	E	F	G	H	I	J	K
I	II	III	IV	V	VI	VII	VIII	IX	X	XI

L	M	N	O	P	Q	R	S
XII	XIII	XIV	XV	XVI	XVII	XVIII	XIX

T	U	V	W	X	Y	Z
XX	XXI	XXII	XXIII	XXIV	XXV	XXVI

Can you decipher this message?

III XV XII XII V III XX
XIII V XIX XIX I VII V
VI XVIII XV XIII   XIX V III XVIII V XX
IV XVIII XV XVI

It reads: COLLECT MESSAGE FROM SECRET DROP.

If you have a dog he can help you in your mission by hiding secret messages for you. If you can train him well enough he might bury secret equipment, or if he is clever his sense of smell might enable him to track down an enemy for you.

An umbrella is always a useful piece of
equipment. It can be used in self-defense if
ever necessary.

A clever way of sending secret messages is to
write your message on the top right hand
corner of an envelope and stick a large stamp
over it. If an enemy intercepts the mail he will
look at the letter inside and find nothing.
Your contact has only to steam the stamp off
the envelope to read the message underneath.

Coloured pencils sticking out of your top
pocket, or different coloured handkerchiefs
can be used successfully to convey messages.

If you are out at night always walk in the
shadows and never directly under street
lamps, otherwise you will be spotted.

If you are trying to crack an enemy code try
counting the frequency of a certain letter. The
letter that occurs most in English is the letter
E, so if a symbol of sign keeps appearing there
is a likelihood that it stands for E. The letter
that appears the second highest number of
times is **T**. Once you have found those two
letters you should find it easier to break the
code.

Here are the rest of the letters in the alphabet
in the order in which they are most used: **A,
O, I, N, R, S, H, D, L, C, U, M, P, F, G,
Y, B, W, K, V, J, Q, X, Z**.

If a fellow agent sneezes loudly three times it
means "**Get out quickly, you've been
spotted**".

There are many signs that can be scratched on the ground to give your contact a signal. They are based on signals usually drawn on the ground in large white letters to pilots in aircraft whose radio contact has broken down.

A letter '**Y**' means '**yes**', '**N**' means '**no**', '**F**' means '**I need food**', and '**LL**' means '**all is well**'.

Look closely for cracks in brick walls or buildings, they could prove to be useful places in which to leave secret messages.

An alternative **Roman Cipher** is to write the Roman Numerals in reverse order, instead of starting at I:

A	B	C	D	E	F
XXVI	XXV	XXIV	XXIII	XXII	XXI

G	H	I	J	K
XX	XIX	XVIII	XVII	XVI

V	W	X	Y	Z
V	IV	III	II	I

The message: **ESCAPE QUICKLY** would read:

XXII VIII XXIV XXVI XI XXII
X VI   XVIII XXIV XVI XV II

Always carry a large white handkerchief with you. Should an emergency arise you can always hide your face in it by pretending to blow your nose.

If you see a large 'X' scratched on to the ground it is a sign from a fellow agent and means '**Do not proceed**'.

To make yourself look fatter you can use rolled up towels as padding, but rather than tie them under your clothes it may sometimes be better to pin or sew them to the inside of the clothes, or inside the lining of your coat. That way there is no danger of the padding slipping and giving you away, and if you need to make a quick change you have only to take off your coat and immediately you will be slim once again.

A realistic looking false nose can be made very easily using plasticine. Roll a piece in your hand to make it warm and soft. Then mould it into the shape of the nose you want, although do not make it too big as it might drop off. Place it over your own nose, not forgetting to leave two nostrils so that you can breathe, and press it on tightly. By looking in a mirror you can get it the correct shape, and to complete the disguise you can cover it with make-up to make it look as realistic as possible. Finally, powder your face and 'nose' to make it blend in completely. Don't forget you must not blow your nose when out on a mission, otherwise it might come off or change shape!

An excellent powder developer for messages written in wax can be bought at most iron-mongers and is called **powdered graphite**. It's real use is for lubricating locks.

Decipher this secret message:

II XII VI   XXIV XXVI XIII
XIII XII IV   XXIV IX XII VIII   VIII
VII XIX XXII
XXV XII IX   XXIII XXII   XI III XXX

It reads: YOU CAN NOW CROSS THE BORDER

If you think you have been spotted, or that an enemy agent is nearby and may spot you, bend down and pretend to tie your shoe lace so that he cannot see your face.

Equipment used in an assassination attempt is known as **ASTRO** equipment. It is rather like a bomb and can be activated by pressure or light.

To practice your skills at tracking it is always useful to study tracks and footprints of all kinds. A valuable piece of equipment is a piece of **cardboard** and some **plaster of Paris** (available from model shops).

If you see an animal track in the ground place a circle of card around it, a paper clip will keep the card together, and pour the made-up plaster into the cardboard and into the track. As it sets put a piece of string into the plaster and this will enable you to hang it up later. After about 30 minutes the plaster will have set hard. Lift it from the ground, clean away any mud, and you should have a perfect plaster cast of the footprint.

The plaster cast of a footprint is called a
'**Negative Cast**' because the print appears like
a bump outwards.

To make a '**Positive Cast**' (which will look
exactly as the print did on the ground) keep
the cardboard around your 'negative cast' and
grease this mould with vaseline or soapy
water, and pour in some Plaster of Paris and
allow it to set. When it is set you can separate
the two halves of the cast. You now have a
perfect print that will last forever and will help
you identify any tracks you see. If you know
which animal made the track, a cat, dog, cow,
horse, fox, badger, or whatever, then label the
cast clearly and gradually you will be able to
build up a whole collection.

Small objects, papers and letters, can easily be
hidden underneath your hat or wig.

The skating rink will provide a superb
opportunity for passing secret messages. On a
skating rink you need to be well wrapped up
with plenty of thick pullovers, coat, scarf,
gloves and hat, which will disguise you. To
pass the message you can pretend to slip over
on the ice and as your contact helps you up
you can pass the message to him.

A special **code grill** can be made very easily.
All you do is take a piece of card and cut out
some holes. Write an ordinary looking letter
which incorporates the words of your message,
with the words strategically placed so that
when the grill is placed over the top just the
words of the message appear.

Disguise your walk by taking very big strides and swinging your arms as you go.

If you measure your arm span, from finger tip to finger tip with your arms stretched as far apart as possible. Once you know the measurement you can use it when you are out on a mission and need to know a specific measurement.

Secret messages can be hidden inside leaves! It sounds difficult, but it's not. Take a large leaf and roll it around a pencil and secure it with an elastic band. Leave the leaf in a box or drawer to dry. When it has dried out you can carefully remove the elastic band and the pencil and the leaf will stay as a hollow tube. Inside you can hide rolled up messages and leave them at a drop. Even if the drop is searched by the enemy they are not going to take any notice of a dried up leaf.

113

If you hide behind a tree and wish to peer round you should do so with just one eye. That way you will not be seen. If you try to look with both eyes your whole head will appear and you will be noticed.

When is a getaway car not a car?

When it turns into a driveway.

If you see a letter K on the ground it is a sign to indicate the direction you should take. It acts as an arrow. **Я**

Strange as it may sound, a wet sponge can be a useful piece of equipment. Keep a small sponge in your pocket in a plastic bag. If you suspect that someone is wearing hand make-up, damp your hand on the sponge slightly and then shake hands with them. If they are wearing make-up it will come off on your hand.

A secret message can be left in one of the holes at a golf course. The courier delivering the message can place the message inside when he reaches to pick out his ball. Likewise, when the contact plays his game he can retrieve the message when he reaches for his ball.

A secret message should be written on a large sheet of paper and that piece of paper should then be made into the shape of an envelope. Inside this envelope you can put a fake letter. If it is intercepted by the enemy they will read the paper inside and would never think of looking on the inside of the envelope.

All trainee spies should go through an assault course to test their skills. One can easily be made from old tyres, blankets, ropes, which will provide obstacles to climb through, under, over, and swing on.

Build up your own files of information by collecting newspaper cuttings of real life spies and spy stories. They could be a useful source of reference.

Carrying a tape measure with you is recommended when trailing an enemy. You can use it to measure footprints and gain some idea of the person's size.

The shape and size of your hands can be changed by wearing rubber household gloves covered with flesh coloured make-up.

You can change the shape of your eyes by cutting a table-tennis ball in half. Make a hole in the middle of each so that you can see through them. Colour them with felt tip pens to look like eyes and wear them.

Knock, knock.
Who's there?
Snow.
Snow who?
Snow use, I've forgotten.

To test your fingerprint skills you can test yourself and members of your spy ring by getting one person to touch a glass. You can then take the fingerprints off with powder and match them up against your records and see whose they are.

To make your teeth looked stained and nasty you can cut yourself a new set out of a piece of orange peel (it is the creamy coloured inside that needs to show) and wear this set over your own teeth. New teeth will also alter the way in which you speak.

Real spies who happen to have false teeth usually have several different sets of teeth which they use when they wish to disguise. One set that gives them protruding front teeth, another set that has some teeth missing and those remaining are stained and chipped, a set of teeth that are quite large, and so on.

If you have studied your enemy agent very carefully you will know if he has any little mannerisms, such as a twitching left eye, a habit of biting his nails, or some such sign which will give him away when he is in disguise. If he has a habit of scratching his nose frequently it will help you track him down when he's in disguise because he will still retain these small mannerisms.

Secret messages can be left very easily at the zoo. They can be left amongst flower beds, or behind a notice. In fact there are a whole host of places. But never slip a message into a cage otherwise your contact is likely to lose an arm trying to retrieve it.

If a fellow agent strokes his chin it means **'meet me later'**.

 Any assumed or false named that an agent adopts is known as an **ALIAS**.

 If you have some strong watertight wellington boots you should wear them when trailing through the country. You can then walk in shallow streams wherever possible and then you will not leave any visible tracks.

The secret of being a good make-up artist and having the very best disguises is to know your own face thoroughly. You may think that you know your own face very well, when in fact you do not. Remember — you are the other side of it so you don't always know what it looks like.

Get to know your face really well by sitting in front of a mirror and making hundreds of different faces. Raise your eyebrows. Try raising just one eyebrow. Give a very big smile. Frown. Make yourself look really sad. Gradually you will get to know the wrinkles and creases of your face, some that you may not have even noticed were there. Use these wrinkles as a guideline to making yourself up.

Occasionally you may only see the enemy agent for a split second, so it is important that you use your powers of observation to the full.

If you suspect that someone is disguising his or her voice try and make them laugh, or jump out on them and give them a fright, and if they are disguising their voice you will soon find out because in those two situations no-one can keep up the pretence.

If you are hiding a secret message on the ground, or between paving stones, roll the paper up and rub some earth on it to camouflage it.

A secret message on a piece of paper can be hidden under a piece of sticking plaster on your arm. If you are ever searched by the enemy they are not going to look under a plaster in case there is a nasty cut underneath.

A person who acts as a go-between for the Master Spy and potential new agents is called a **Cut-Out**. This is not a dangerous job because the Cut-Out never has access to any information so he has nothing to hide.

Signs that appear on clear nights to show you the way are the stars.

If your mission involves some research into history do not be fooled into believing that something happened on **10th September 1752**, because it didn't! Believe it or not that day simply did not exist! This is because on the 2nd September 1752 the calendar was changed and jumped straight ahead to the 14th September. So, you will now know that there are twelve days in history on which absolutely nothing happened!

If a spy puts his hands on his hips it means **'send your report to the Master Spy immediately.'**

Make it look as if you have injured your head by wrapping a bandage around it. To make it look worse you can even bring the bandage down to cover one eye.

One code that is often used as a hand signal with flags is called **Semaphore**, but it can also be used as a written code too. The symbols are well known, as are the Morse Code symbols, but you can vary them. Below are the symbols in the form of a clock face:

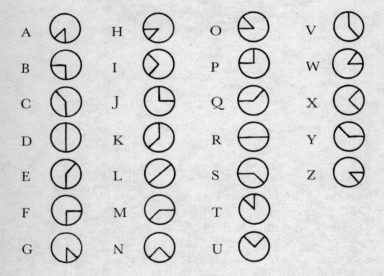

So the word **ESPIONAGE** would be written like this:

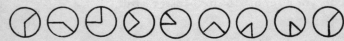

The position of the hands on the clock can be copied with your arms using flags if you wish to use the Semaphore code as a proper signal. Remember to keep your arms prefectly straight all the time.

Can you decipher this secret message?

It reads: DANGER

A secret message can often be tucked inside or pinned to the belt of a coat. If you are searched the enemy is likely to look in the pockets and the lining, even under the collar or behind the lapels, but is unlikely to look at the belt.

An illuminated magnifying glass, such as sold at many garages and car accessory shops, will prove to be much better than an ordinary magnifying glass when studying maps or finger prints because it will make the subject much clearer to see.

Always mix invisible inks, especially chemical inks, in an old jam jar or disposable container. NEVER mix them in a drinking glass otherwise you are likely to get poisoned.

If leaving special signs do not leave more than are necessary otherwise they will be spotted by the enemy and may even confuse your contact.

A piece of ordinary garden cane, such as are used to prop up and support flowers and plants, can prove useful places for hiding secret messages. Take a screw-driver to make the hole in the centre larger and hollow the middle out. Having done this you can then roll your message up very tightly and slip it into the cane.

Disguise your voice by talking with a regional accent. Practice some of the following: Scottish; Yorkshire; Welsh; Norfolk; Devonshire; Somerset; Cornish; Wiltshire; Irish; Lancashire.

What did the Irish spy say to the chiropidist?

My fate is in your hands.

Secret messages can be cellotaped to the back of watches and worn on your wrist.

A good disguise is that of an old lady. An old coat, skirt and hat are all you need. A wig or talcum powder can be used to grey your hair, and a few lines drawn in the creases of your face to make you look old. Whilst in disguise you can sit on a park bench and knit whilst observing the enemy.

Cut out as many colour pictures of faces from magazines as you can and cut them up so that you seperate the mouths, eyes, noses, hair, and ears. You can then use them to build up indentikit pictures of any suspects. If you cannot find many pictures then you can always draw them on to strips of card.

In his book *A Tale of Two Cities* Charles Dickens created a character called Madame Defarge who used to sit and knit beside the guillotine during the French Revolution whilst heads were being cut off. Her knitting, however, was a form of passing secret messages for the various stitches she used were her very own secret code.

If you happen to be studying the footprints of your quarry and notice that they are slightly deeper on one side it generally indicates that he is carrying something heavy.

Spies should be fashion conscious and should be able to look very smart when mixing in elegant circles. If the occasion calls for a top hat then this can be used to hide cameras and small pieces of equipment underneath.

 A hollow tree can be an excellent hideout if it is large enough for you to get inside and remain completely hidden. Look around for any holes which you can see through, and wear camouflage on your hat so that you can lift your head out without being spotted.

Use plasticine or special nose putty to make bumps, warts, and spots on your skin. Cover them with make-up to blend them in with your own skin so that they look realistic.

Two crossed twigs, or a broken twig is a sign meaning '**Do not go any further**'.

No two people have the same fingerprints. Even those of identical twins are different. So once you have collected a person's fingerprints and you have them on record you will always be able to use them to identify that person.

A very elegant spy whilst dining at the Savoy hotel or whilst at a Buckingham Palace garden party will have a secret message hidden inside a long cigarette holder.

To avoid suspicion spies should, wherever possible, walk around in pairs. They can then chat quite happily and nobody will take any notice of them.

Look for statues and monuments in your town. They often have small cracks in the pedestal or a gap somewhere in the stonework in which a secret message can be hidden. If the statue is a tourist attraction your contact can collect the message by posing as a tourist.

The waiting room of a railway or bus station is a useful hiding and meeting place. Spies can sit and discuss plans, or just sit and observe people. No-one will know that you are not waiting for a bus or train.

What does a spy do when an enemy's nose is running?

Put his foot out and trip it up.

No spy would ever betray his network, but if you are ever captured pretend betrayal by giving them false secrets and fake secret messages and codes.

Do not worry if a false beard does not match your own hair exactly. If you look at people with real beards you will see that they are rarely the same colour as the hair on their head.

In China, spies have special typewriters which are like two machines joined together. You type your message on one machine and it comes out typed in code on the other. It is possible for cipher clerks to type out a message and not even see what the coded message looks like. This way as few people as possible know about it. The machines can also be used in reverse if a message in code is typed out on the other machine the decoded message will come out of the other. Again, this can be performed by a cipher clerk who may never see the decoded message.

If no invisible inks are available you can use the **watermark method**. Soak a sheet of paper in water and lay it flat on a sheet of glass or a mirror. Place a sheet of dry paper on the top and write your message in pencil or with a ball point pen. Having written your message destroy the top copy and allow the bottom piece of paper to dry. When it is dry it will look like a perfectly ordinary piece of plain paper **but** if you wet it again the message will appear on the paper like a watermark, and will disappear once more when the paper dries.

Beware of any mirrors in a room, they could be two-way mirrors and someone could be watching you.

A useful piece of equipment is called an **Oscillograph**. It can be attached to a telephone and record the numbers of any callers. Very useful if an enemy attempts to ring you anonymously because you will be able to trace where he is ringing from.

If someone leaves your spy ring and moves to the enemy side he is known as a **Defector**.

If offered a drink containing an olive always squeeze the olive because it could contain a bug. If you discover a bug you can deactivate it by pulling off the antennae.

Powdered lead can be used to dust finger-prints. You can then mount them on white paper.

 To make a nasty looking bump on your arm or leg put a piece of sticking plaster over a lump of cotton wool.

 A triangle of sticks or stones on the ground means '**Proceed with caution**'.

To disguise your voice on the telephone talk with a pencil between your teeth.

Ultra-violet light, sometimes known as black-light, can be used to detect enemy messages written in invisible ink.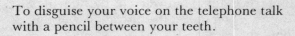

If you have to talk to your contact on the telephone always speak clearly and spell any words that might be misunderstood. To do this there is a special **International call-up alphabet** that is used all over the world. For example, if you had to spell out the word **SUSPECT** you would say:

SIERRA — UNCLE — SIERRA — PAPA — ECHO — CHARLIE — TANGO

Here is the international alphabet:

A	**ALPHA**	N	**NOVEMBER**
B	**BRAVO**	O	**OSCAR**
C	**CHARLIE**	P	**PAPA**
D	**DELTA**	Q	**QUEBEC**
E	**ECHO**	R	**ROMEO**
F	**FOXTROT**	S	**SIERRA**
G	**GOLF**	T	**TANGO**
H	**HOTEL**	U	**UNCLE**
I	**INDIA**	V	**VICTOR**
J	**JULIET**	W	**WHISKY**
K	**KILO**	X	**X-RAY**
L	**LIMA**	Y	**YANKEE**
M	**MIKE**	Z	**ZULU**

To test your tracking skills practice on a wet beach with a friend. Footprints will show up quite clearly in the sand. Study the soles of your friends shoes. Close your eyes and let him 'escape' after 3-4 minutes open your eyes and try and find out where is by studying his tracks. Then repeat the operation, but this time you escape.

If a fellow spy scratches his right ear it means **'Someone is listening to us'**.

To disguise your voice try talking with your tongue either in front or behind your bottom teeth and you will find it gives you a completely new voice.

It is essential that a secret agent is fit, so when you wake up each morning go to the window and take several deep breaths. Really fill your lungs with oxygen, hold your breath for a few seconds, and then release. This will get your lungs working correctly and will give you energy for the day.

Voice activated bugs are special pieces of equipment that can be attached to an ordinary tape recorder and only work when someone speaks. This means that on a tape you will only have people's conversations and there will not be long gaps and wasted tape whilst people were out of the room.

Semaphore flags can be made with two pieces of cane, or an old broom handle cut in half. Staple or sew on to this stick a piece of red cloth, Make two identical flags and you will then be able to send proper semaphore messages.

To completely fool your enemy place a book on your book shelves clearly marked *Secret Code Book* and fill it with meaningless letters and symbols.

Using the invention of a micro-dot a page of information can be reduced to the size of a dot over a letter **i** and placed on an innocent looking page where it will never be detected.

To discover if you have a double-agent in your network give him a secret that is totally untrue. If you discover later that the enemy know this secret you will know that a double agent is amongst you.

When in disguise you should carry a handkerchief with false initials embroidered on it.

Always carry a diary with a false name and false address in it. This will fool the enemy if you are captured.

In a crowded room you can signal to a fellow agent with a silent signal. A scratch on the head could mean '**you are being watched**'.

 A **dead letter box** can be a hollow tree, under a stone, or anywhere that a piece of paper can be concealed.

 If a fellow spy blows his nose it means '**keep an eye on the door**'.

 If you keep a magnetised needle under your lapel it will be with you at all times and can be used as a compass if you get lost.

Make-up must always be practised in front of a mirror in secret.

If you draw lines on your face with an eyebrow pencil these will make you look much older.

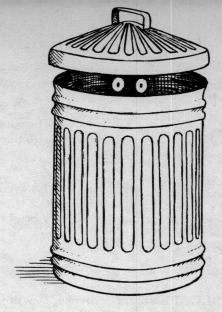

 An empty dustbin will provide a useful hiding place for a spy if it has some holes drilled into it for you to see out of. Never hide inside a dustbin with a lid on as this could be very dangerous. A dustman could easily carry you off thinking you were rubbish. The secret is to crouch down low so that you are not seen, and without the lid you will be able to make a very quick escape.

The pad of a dog's foot print is usually triangular, whilst a cat's is round.

You can give yourself a rosier complexion by rubbing rouge into your cheeks.

 In **DOUBLE SPEAK** (the language of spies) the sentence '**It is sunny today**' means '**There are a lot of enemies about.**'

131

To make your face look paler dab it gently with talcum powder.

Experiment with eye-shadow. It can make your eyes look sunken or very bright.

In **DOUBLE SPEAK** the sentence 'It will rain later today' means 'There will be a meeting this evening.'

Always place something in your shoe when you want to fake a limp otherwise you might forget which foot you are limping with and the enemy will soon spot that you are a fake.

If you develop a leaf code of your own bend over a leaf a push the stalk through the top of it — so that a tube is made. This could mean '**Danger ahead**'.

Try and go to school a different way each morning so that the enemy cannot predict your movements.

To avoid suspicion when wearing binoculars disguise yourself as a naturalist and then nobody will take any notice of you.

If you hide behind the curtains in the enemy headquarters and it is day-time the curtains will be open, so stand very straight and completely still behind one of the curtains.

A fake cut on your hand can be made to look even worse if you draw some stitches across it with a black felt-tip pen. Enough to make the enemy faint on the spot.

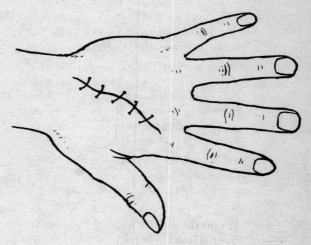

In leaf code, a small twig push through the centre of a leaf could mean 'meet me tonight as arranged'.

If you hide behind the curtains in a room and someone approaches you, or there is a chance that you might be detected, then you can make a quick escape through the window.

Small messages can be tucked inside a picture frame.

If a horse is shod then his tracks will be easily seen and will be very different to any other animal.

Always leave the house at different times and in disguise so that the enemy can never predict your movements.

Any good spy will know of the existence of micro-rockets so if you carry a drinking straw with you at all times if captured by the enemy you can pretend that you are going to fire a rocket at him by getting out your straw. He will be so scared that you will be able to escape.

Never have a meeting at your school if two members of your spy ring go to another school as they will miss out on the meeting.

A secret code book can be made from absolutely any book and as long as you and your contact each have a copy of the same book you will be able to send secret messages. Simply find the words of your message in the book and give the page number, the number of the line (starting from the top of the page), and the number of words from the left along the line. All you have to do is find the page and count, for example, seven lines down and the third word along on page 23 for the first word of the message.

A message will look like this:

**32.10.2   71.14.9   63.7.1   77.13.8
62.12.3   10.2.1**

Remember, the sequence should be: **Page — Line — Word**. Unless your contact knows that he might get the wrong message!

Always select a meeting place where you cannot be overheard.

Keep your secret things in a box that is marked '**Table Tennis Balls**' or '**Crayons**', then if the enemy search your headquarters they will not bother looking inside it.

Always have a spy meeting in a place that is convenient for everyone.

Always have two identification documents for each spy in your ring. One with their true identity and one that contains fake details and false information about them. Keep the genuine documents very carefully hidden and leave the fakes in a place where the enemy would soon find them if they came searching your hideout.

If you are having a meeting at the library then tell your parents that you are going to the library. Don't say the library if you are meeting at the youth club because someone somewhere will spot you and your cover will be blown.

Telephone conversations can be recorded by connecting a tape-recorder to a telephone. If someone rings you place the microphone against the earpiece of your receiver and record the conversation.

If secret messages are hidden inside clocks then care must be taken not to damage the clock in any way, otherwise someone is sure to look inside and your secret will no longer be safe.

A sling on your arm can provide a very useful hiding place for a small tape recorder.

A hat can make a useful hiding place and will also act as a disguise.

Modern devices are miniature bugs which can be used to tap telephone conversations. They can be inserted inside the earpiece of a telephone and the mini transmitter will then transmit all conversations to the spy's headquarters.

 If you take a drawer out of a chest or sideboard you can often find a small cavity at the back which could prove to be an invaluable hiding place for small objects.

 To improve your skill at code breaking try playing a game of Scrabble using a particular code.

 Secret messages and small objects can often be hidden behind cushions or down the back of armchairs.

A cipher in which a plain letter, symbol, figure or number is substituted for each letter of the alphabet is called a **Substitution Cipher**.

A cipher in which all the letters of the message are left the same but the order is jumbled up is called a **Transposition Cipher**. A few null letters are sometimes added to make it harder to break.

Making an invisible message appear is known as **DEVELOPING**.

There are many exercises you can undertake to test your memory. One simple method is to get someone to show you a tray with twenty objects on it. Study the tray for two minutes only. Then, without looking at the tray, say or write down everything that you remember seeing.

Papers and maps can be hidden under mattresses and carpets.

 If there is any stress in someone's voice it usually means that they are not telling the truth.

 If you are hiding in an enemy hotel room and there is a double bed then it might be safer for **two** of your agents to hide underneath.

 If a hotel room has a single bed only but two agents need to hide then one can conceal himself in the wardrobe.

If you are on the beach a sun hat and a pair of dark glasses will make you unrecognisable, because you will look just like everybody else.

A secret message can be hidden in the hollow cone of an ice-cream cornet. You can pass it to your contact easily without arousing suspicion.

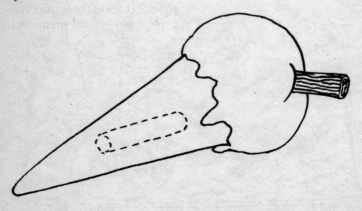

If you have to communicate with a contact on the beach he can lie beside you in the sand behind a wind-shield and you can whisper to each other or use pebbles as signals to pass on secret messages.

If you are hiding a small object inside a tin of talcum powder, wrap it in cotton wool so that it will not rattle if someone shakes the tin.

A realistic birthmark can be made on your face by using an eyebrow pencil to draw a distinctive mark. The enemy will then be looking for a birthmark so that they can recognise you in future.

When you write letters that have a message in invisible ink hidden between the lines be sure to end your fake letter with your own special code to let your contact know what it has been written with. If you end the letter *'yours sincerely'* it means lemon juice has been used; *'yours truly'* means milk was used; *'yours faithfully'* that a sugar and water solution was used; and *'very sincerely yours'* could mean that Copper Sulphate was used.

To devise your own code write down the alphabet and then get each member of your spy ring to think of different symbols for each. Providing each member of your ring then learns the code you will have a unique method of communication that even an experienced cipher clerk will have difficulty in breaking.

When a fellow spy folds his arms it means '**I need protection**'.

A girl can disguise herself as a boy, either by
wearing a short wig, or by tying her hair
back. She could wear trousers and a jacket,
and perhaps even give herself a moustache
and dark glasses to make the transformation
complete.

 Always have a first-aid kit in your spy
headquarters in case of any emergency. Have
inside some antiseptic cream, sticking plasters,
plenty of cotton wool, and a crepe bandage.

 Knock, knock.
Who's there?
Ivor.
Ivor who?
Ivor you let me in the door or I'll climb
through the window.

 When you wake up each morning stretch each
muscle in turn, raising your arms and legs up
towards the ceiling. This will wake you up and
make you feel fully alert.

When you leave your hideout always wipe the
door handle or knob with a cloth. On your
return you can test for fingerprints to see if
anyone has tried the handle.

American spies write messages in fluorescent invisible ink. The message can only be read when an ultra-violet light is shone onto the paper.

A spy who is good at knitting or embroidery can develop a secret code of his or her own in which different series and sequences of knots and stitches can convey a whole message. An innocent looking scarf could contain a highly secret piece of information.

Liquid developers for invisible messages can be sprayed from an ordinary spray, such as the kind used for perfume which are re-fillable.

Goat's milk and evaporated milk make just as good an invisible ink as cow's milk.

The earth rotates at a speed of 29 km a minute.

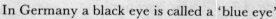

In Germany a black eye is called a 'blue eye'

Watch television plays and see how any actors that you know well have changed their voice, mannerisms, and appearance, it might give you a few tips when you are disguising yourself.

Which is the most shocking city in the world?

Electri-city.

23% of the world's population speak Chinese.

Always carry a pair of tweezers with you for picking up any small clues, such as human hair that might help you to identify an enemy agent.

A realistic scar can be drawn on your face with a thin red line, and can be made to look deeper if you blend some white eye-liner along the edge.

Secret codes are used by the Government when sending important messages to Ambassadors in foreign countries, even in peacetime.

What part of the army could a baby join?

The infantry.

A spy should practise sketching faces, he can then draw pictures of suspects while they are still fresh in his mind.

Practise sketching techniques by copying pictures from magazines. You can then look at a picture, close the magazine, and try to draw the features of the person as accurately as possible.

Another reliable compass, using a magnetised needle as before, can be made by placing a leaf or piece of tissue paper on to some water so that it floats. Carefully lay the needle on to the leaf. Now, very carefully indeed push the leaf under the water. The needle should remain afloat and will swing round to point north. Practise in a dish of water at your headquarters.

Bumps can be made from nose putty and
blended in with make-up.

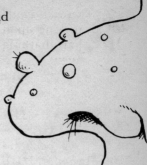

Ex-spy: "I can keep a
secret. It's the people I
tell it to who can't!"

When you are out in the street test your
powers of observation by looking at the way
people walk, how they stand when they are
not doing anything, how two people behave
when they are talking to each other, how they
dress, what they carry, and jot down any
notes that will be useful for the future.

If you look in a book of invisible inks and see
the words **F** or **P** beside it these letters stand
for 'fugitive' and 'permanent'.

Fugitive means that you will have to warm
the paper to read the message and once the
paper has cooled it will disappear again.

Permanent means that once you have
developed the message the writing will remain
visible, such as if you put powder on a
message in wax.

You can invent your own code of coloured
dots and put them on used matchsticks. They
can be left lying around to convey messages to
fellow agents.

In the privacy of your own room, practise some of the walks that you have seen in the street. Pretend that you are waiting for a bus or taxi, and copy the different ways in which you have observed people standing.

Using the **Double-Dutch Cipher** place the word **UK** after every consonant in your word. CAT becomes **CUKATUK** and DOG becomes **DUKOGUK**.

A secret message can be sent by placing the syllables **IP** after each consonant in your word. So, the word DOG becomes **DIPOGIP**, and CAT becomes **CIPATIP**, and so on.

A **consonant** is a letter of the alphabet which cannot be sounded by itself, such as **b** or **p** — a sound that is combined with a vowel to make a syllable.

Create your own Double-Dutch Ciphers by creating your own syllables, such as **OP, OD, AT, IK**, etc. and placing them after consonants in your message.

To develop secret messages written in wax place some powdered graphite in a little cloth bag and rub the bag gently over the paper. The message will then appear.

Develop your own code with coloured handkerchiefs. A red handkerchief in your top pocket could mean **danger**, green could mean **all is well**, etc.

If you carry an umbrella with you it can be lowered to cover your face whenever necessary so that no enemy agent will be able to spot who is behind it.

An umbrella is a useful piece of equipment, for if it is raining it will protect your disguise and prevent any make-up from washing off.

A pet dog can be used as a method of carrying secret messages. Tuck a message under his collar and take him for a walk in the park. When you meet your contact he can bend down to pat the dog, and whilst stroking him can skillfully remove the message at the same time.

Coloured pencils in your pocket can be used to convey messages. Use different combinations of colours for each message, so that, for example, a red, yellow and blue pencil in your top pocket will mean '**follow me back to headquarters**'.

When you have mastered the art of codes and ciphers you can develop your own code in which one single word replaces a whole sentence.

 Using code words **SAUSAGES** could mean '**Meet at the hideout**', whereas **FRIED SAUSAGES** might mean '**Meet at the main headquarters**'.

An enemy cipher clerk can be completely baffled if you not only reduce whole sentences to single code words, but if you also send the code word in a cipher. Hence, if given this message — **20 1 22 20 1 7 5 20** — your agent would know that it was the code word SAUSAGES in a number cipher and he would soon get the message.

A piece of equipment commonly used in foreign spy circles is a device which can be attached to a telephone. When the receiver is lifted the device explodes in five seconds.

Dry Ice does not melt like ordinary ice, it evaporates and looks just like smoke. It can be used to make a 'smoke screen' whilst you escape from the enemy.

If you have built an assault course in your garden to test the skills of your spies, try simulating the conditions of war by playing tape-recorded sounds of battle noises whilst your trainees go through the course.

If you do not possess a tape-recorder but wish to have battle sounds to test your agents then get the other members of your spy ring to make the noises themselves.

Effective gunshot sounds can be simulated by bursting an inflated paper bag.

If you carry a comic around with you, not only can you read it when you have time to kill, you can sit on it if the ground is damp.

147

 When experimenting with make-up don't just try and make yourself look beautiful, or old, but use the make-up sometimes to see if you can make yourself as ugly as possible.

 False eyes made from two halves of a ping-pong ball can be worn behind ordinary glasses. The glasses will keep the 'eyes' in place and will aid you in your disguise.

If you have any small mannerisms, such as biting your nails, then take note of them and try to change them when you are in disguise. It could be that you, for example, walk with your feet pointing outwards and this could easily give you away.

148

It is very difficult to disguise your laugh, so listen carefully to people's laughs so that you can recognise them, even when in disguise.

Test your powers of observation by looking at a magazine picture of a man for two seconds. Close the magazine and try and write down exactly what he was wearing, the colour of his eyes, hair, whether he had a beard, moustache, glasses, etc., also what he was carrying, what he was wearing on his feet, and any distinguishing marks. Then look back at the picture and see how good your observation was.

Test your memory by looking at a photograph, or a person in the street for two seconds, and then try and build up an identikit picture of him.

Polaris (the Northern Star) will always tell you which direction is north.

A visit to your local library to do some research on astronomy is time well spent. It will prevent you losing your way at night.

A little tomato sauce on a bandage will make it look as if you have had a particularly nasty accident, and a secret document can be hidden underneath the bandage, because no one will dare look there!

An ordinary piece of garden cane can be used to convey secret messages if secret signs and symbols are scratched down the edge.

Try mastering various different accents then you can disguise yourself as one of the locals in a particular area of the country and speak like a 'native'.

American secret agents take the insides out of old watches. This leaves a hollow compartment inside in which micro-film or any small object can remain hidden and strapped to their wrist.

Gloves are the only method of disguising fingerprints.

Sometimes hardened criminals have plastic surgery on their fingertips to avoid detection, but they have still been caught because the print they leave is still unique.

By disguising as an historian a spy can hide behind old gravestones, pretending that he is collecting information. He can also collect any secret messages hidden in cracks on statues and monuments.

The tongue prints of cows
are unique, just like
our fingerprints. No two cows
have the same tongue print.

A secret message can be hidden quite easily in
the knot of a scarf or pinned behind a bow tie.

If you find a deep crack in any stonework you
should attach a piece of string to your
message, push the paper deep into the crack,
and leave just a small piece of string hanging
out. Your contact has then only to pull the
string and he has the message.

The most important skill of a spy is always to
see without ever being **seen**.

A piece of garden cane or a stick that is
supporting some flowers can have a message
in Morse Code put on it if you draw a series
of dots and dashes down one edge.

Anyone disguised as a gardener can easily
collect messages on garden canes by
pretending to tend to the flowers.

Fingerprints can be dusted with talcum
powder and mounted on black paper.

If you hide amongst the crowds at a bus or railway station you will be able to see if any enemy agents from other countries are arriving in your town.

If you are observing people at a bus or railway station and are spotted by an enemy agent you can always jump on the next bus home and make a quick escape.

If one of your agents defects to the enemy side you must change all your codes, hideouts, drops, and equipment, otherwise he will pass your secrets on to the enemy.

 Miniature bugs and listening devices can be hidden in a bowl of sugar without being seen.

 A spy should pay careful attention to his diet, never skip meals, and get plenty of exercise.

If you suspect that someone has planted a voice activated bug in your room (a tape-recorder that only works when someone speaks) simply put on the radio or television and this will soon use up all the tape. The enemy will soon get bored of listening to the radio.

 If you want a brief conversation with an agent and think someone is listening then put on the radio or a record very loudly and then whisper in the agent's ear.

 Semaphore flags can be made using two sticks and two handkerchiefs if you have nothing else.

Minature listening devices can be sewn into the hem of the curtains at your enemy headquarters.

Sport is a very good way of keeping fit, so after spy meetings try and have a period of relaxation and play a team game.

Try and find yourself a good strong metal box. An old biscuit tin will be ideal. Inside it can be put codebooks and any documents that must never be found. Bury the box in the garden where it is unlikely to be found.

When on a mission in the country you can disguise yourself as a scarecrow. Wear some old clothes. A battered hat with some straw hair. Practise standing very still.

A wooden rod or cane will be a useful piece of equipment if disguised as a scarecrow. Simply push it though the sleeves of your jacket, across your back, and it will support your arms. A broom handle is ideal.

If you are really desperate for a disguise have a look through the Yellow Pages of your telephone directory. This will give you addresses of Theatrical Costumiers and Fancy Dress Hire firms. You can then go along and get some ideas.

What sort of robber is the easiest?

A safe robbery.

If you find yourself in the jungle there is no need to be frightened of a gorilla — although he may look very fierce he is strictly vegetarian.

Keep a strong cardboard box or suitcase as your disguise box. Every time you collect a piece of clothing put it in this box until it is needed.

Someone who helps a criminal is called an **ACCESSORY**.

The soil in a pot plant can provide a useful hiding place for miniature bugs.

Always make certain that you have a watch that keeps very good time. It is essential that a spy arrives everywhere on time, so keep a constant check.

To search an enemy agent for weapons is known as **FRISKING**.

Why did the bald spy throw away his keys?

Because he didn't have any locks.

154

Alexander the Great had several very large helmets made, which were left lying around in the hope that the enemy would think his army was made up of giants.

Collect as many newspaper cuttings and magazine articles as you can on real life spies and keep them in a file, these could be a useful source of reference.

To make a bump appear on your arm or leg put a piece of sticking plaster over a lump of cotton wool. Cover the sticking plaster with make-up to make it look red and swollen, or even bruised.

Carry a notebook and pencil with you at all times. You never know when you may want to jot down notes.

Never leave any gaps in your spy notebook as someone could easily fill in some false information to fool you.

A general message to all the spies in your ring is called an APB, which means an 'All points bulletin'.

Stage blood can be purchased from most joke shops. If you let some trickle over a fake cut it will make it look quite recent.

If you are checking a car for clues take a careful look at the tyres for pieces of tar, mud, straw or pebbles may be stuck between the treads and give you some idea where it has just come from.

155

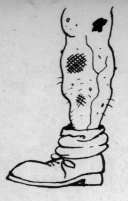

Legs can be made to look veined and nasty by
drawing lines with a felt-tipped pen onto a
pair of flesh coloured tights. Any bruises or
blemishes that you paint onto the tights will
look as if they are actually on your leg.

Big X: I'm looking for a spy with one eye
called Bond.
BIG Q: *What's the other eye called?*

If you find a deep shoeprint in soft mud you
can still take a plaster cast of it. Spray the
print with a little hairspray. Mix some Plaster
of Paris with water and two tablespoons of
sugar and pour it straight into the print.
When the plaster is dry you can lift it out of
the mud and you will have an exact copy of
the shoe sole.

The symbol for a dollar is a modified version
of the symbol stamped on the old Spanish
'pieces of eight'.

To disguise your voice and appearance put a
wad of clean cotton wool or lint between your
teeth and lips over your gums.

156

Doctor: You need glasses.
Spy: *How do you know?*
Doctor: I could tell as soon as you walked through the window.

Although no two fingerprints are identical they can nevertheless be divided into four groups.

Here are the four basic types of fingerprint:

a) **Loops —** the lines all bend in a loop, like a hairpin.

b) **Whorls —** there is a complete circle in the centre, surrounded by more circles.

c) **Arches —** there is an arch at the centre and the lines around it curve in the same way.

d) **Composite —** a mixture of types.

Don't put padding in your mouth if you need to talk very much.

Look carefully at people's hands as the enemy may forget that these will look the same when in disguise. Look especially for any rings.

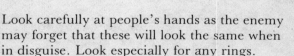

Get to know your face by sitting in front of a mirror in a darkened room and shine a torch on your face from all different angles and see how the different highlights change your appearance. This will help you when making up.

Watch as many detective films and read as many 'whodunnit' novels as you can, you may pick up some very useful tips.

The way in which an enemy works when doing evil things is called **MO** by the police, this is Latin for **modus operandi** or **method of operation**.

The human brain uses the same power as a 10 watt bulb.

Always dab your make-up with powder. This will prevent your face from looking shiny and unnatural. Be sure to close your eyes when dabbing powder on your face.

Always place a mirror in front of a window when you want to make-up as this will light your face completely from all angles.

How does a spy dress on a cold day?

Very quickly.

158

If a spy digs a hole in the middle of a road what will come up?

A policeman.

The most famous fictional detective of all time is undoubtedly **Sherlock Holmes** created by Sir Arthur Conan Doyle who waged a constant war against his arch-enemy Moriarty. Try reading two of his most popular books **The Hound of the Baskervilles** and **A Study in Scarlet**, for a spy can learn a great deal from detective novels.

From a chemist **tincture of iodine** can be obtained. When diluted with water it makes an excellent invisible ink.

If a captured enemy agent blinks a lot when being questioned there is a good chance that he is not telling the truth.

When deciphering messages remember that more than 50% of all words in the English language begin with the letters T, O, A, S, and W.

In the Arctic an ordinary conversation can be heard 3.6 kilometres away. So beware!

Keep all your make-up in a metal box, ideally a large biscuit tin. You can put compartments inside with strips of cardboard to keep it neat.

Modern instant cameras are now quite cheap and are invaluable pieces of modern technology, enabling you to have your photograph within seconds.

When developing secret messages by heat **NEVER** place them near anything that is connected with electricity. This could be very dangerous.

A good hiding place for secret documents or pieces of equipment is inside an empty milk bottle. Paint it outside with white gloss paint. When dry it will look like a full bottle. An ordinary milkbottle top can then be placed on the top. Anything can then be hidden inside and could be left on a doorstep for your contact to collect or even inside a refrigerator.

Avoid very heavy make-up as it will look very false.

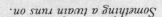

What's a twack?

Something a twain runs on.

When writing secret messages with chemical invisible inks **NEVER** attempt to mix two chemicals together.

When developing secret messages you must use the correct developer otherwise you may lose the message altogether.

 If you are being trailed by an enemy agent try and visit a waxworks. Having lost him or her in the crowd you can then stand very still and pretend to be a waxwork dummy.

 Why wouldn't the Master Spy's bicycle stand up on its own?

Because it was two tyred.

To walk as though you are old place your feet approximately 30 cm apart.

Test your agents' tracking powers by laying a trail for them to follow.

The three-toed sloth disguises itself by allowing its body to be covered by a layer of tiny plants.

If you are being trailed, visit a friend's house. While the enemy agent is waiting outside for you to come out escape through the back door.

 To give yourself bulging muscles wrap a rectangular pad around your arm just above the elbow and put your clothes over the top.

 In spy jargon diamonds are sometimes called **SPARKLERS**.

To alter the appearance of your hands try attaching some false fingernails. These can be bought in many joke shops or in chemists complete with the correct kind of adhesive. Never use ordinary glue otherwise they will be on your fingers forever!

Carry a coat with you. If you are spotted, put it on, it will make you look different.

Ice cream does not cool you, it actually makes you warmer.

If you pull all your books to the front of your bookshelves it will leave a space at the back behind which many small objects can be hidden.

Anyone who is paid to give information is called a **STOOLIE**.

You can tell if a watch is very old because the roman numerals for the number 4 are expressed as IIII and not IV as on more recent clocks and watches.

During the French Revolution a midget was used as a spy and was carried through the enemy lines disguised as a baby.

If a spy has both hands in his pockets it means **'All is well and under control'**.

Disguised as a magazine reporter you can attempt to interview the enemy agent by telling him that you will make him into a big cover star.

It takes 43 muscles to frown, but only 17 to smile.

Dark shading down each side of the nose will make your nose look very long and thin.

A clever secret code is called **OPISH**, in which the letters OP are placed after every consonant. The word BOY becomes **BOPOYOP** and GIRL becomes **GOPIROPLOP**.

Miniature **button bugs** look like an ordinary shirt button and can be sewn on to a shirt or blouse. When you are out on a mission your headquarters will be able to keep in touch with all that you are doing and hear all the conversations you have.

When laying a test trail use a piece of chalk and use a series of pre-arranged signs to show your agents the way.

In the year 500 BC a secret agent called Trimalcio set out on a mission, leaving behind him a trail of seeds so that he could find his way back — or if he got into danger his contacts could follow the trail themselves which would lead them to him. Unfortunately Trimalcio was captured by the enemy and the seeds were eaten by wild birds. Trimalcio was never seen again.

Never leave a trail or spy sign made out of anything edible, otherwise some wild animal is sure to eat it. Leave signs using twigs or pebbles.

What did the spy get when he crossed a carrier pigeon with a woodpecker?

A bird that knocked before it delivered the message.

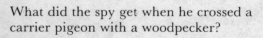
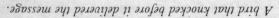

If you have a round face try shading the sides of your face to make it look long and thin.

Cat's eyes appear to glow in the dark because they reflect the light.

Strawberry jam diluted with a little water makes an excellent ink.

Ordinary flesh coloured sticking plaster can alter your natural features beyond recognition.

Give yourself an oriental look by changing the shape of your eyelids with an eyebrow pencil.

Practise walking around your house as silently as possible, learning how to cope with creaky floorboards.

Take care never to spill invisible inks onto your clothing or onto the carpet.

A copy of the *Highway Code* should be kept at your headquarters so that spies can learn it. Once you know all the signs, you can, for example, prevent yourself taking a road that is a dead-end.

Castor oil is the best natural oil in the world.

Why did the chicken cross
the road?

For some foul reason.

Always keep a copy of your code book hidden
in a very secret place. If you lost or
accidentally destroyed the original you would
still have a copy.

Miniature bugs and listening devices can be
sewn into the hem of a table-cloth. If your
enemies sit around the table to discuss plans
you will hear all.

Always keep your passport in a very safe place
and take a note of the number. If it was lost
you would not be able to leave the country on
a mission.

Once you have discovered a good disguise
write down the details on a piece of paper and
file it for future reference — which sticks of
make-up you wear where and so on.

166

Draw a map of your area on a large piece of cardboard, and using the pieces from a Monopoly game put in all the houses and buildings.

In cold weather secret messages can be rolled into a tube and carried in one of the fingers of a glove.

Theatrical make-up sticks were invented by Ludwig Leichner.

The Leichner make-up company produce many different charts which are rather like maps and show you exactly how to make-up into a particular character.

A secret message can be written on a piece of paper and then painted over with white **Snowpake** that typists use to cover mistakes. To read the message the paper should be held up to the light.

In winter secret messages can be carried inside a muffler.

When making yourself look old don't forget to lighten your eyebrows.

What happened to the spy who couldn't tell putty from porridge?

His windows fell out.

Always keep a calendar so that you can plan ahead, marking on school holidays and other important events.

Plaster casts of very small objects can be made quite easily. Simply press the object carefully into a lump of plasticine and then remove it. You should be left with the shape of the object imprinted in the plasticine. Fill the hole with Plaster of Paris and allow to set. You will then have a perfect copy in plaster of your object.

Human beings die more quickly from lack of sleep than lack of food.

Many modern air-freshners are made in unusual shapes and can be attached to doors and walls. They can look rather like mini-microphones so leave one lying around your headquarters — it will frighten away intruders and freshen up your office.

If you have no make-up a piece of burnt cork will do just as well and can be used to give yourself a 'black eye' or a very nasty looking bruise.

Bright coloured posters or wrapping paper can be put on the walls of your headquarters to decorate the place and secret messages can be sellotaped behind them.

Keep a fake calendar hanging on the wall to fool the enemy. *'Out all day'* can be written on a day when you intend to be in, and you can see what happens!

Test your agents' abilities at decoding messages by having a race to see who can break a code first.

I have five noses, six ears, and four eyes, what am I?

Very ugly!

Secret documents can be hidden inside pillow-cases on your pillows.

There are nearly 450 mosques in Istanbul, so do not say to a contact 'I'll meet you by the mosque' as you could spend a week looking for the right one.

When making your face up to look old don't forget to make your neck up, too.

When you de-code messages **accuracy** is more important than **speed**.

The chemical name for the salt we eat is **Chloride of Sodium**.

If you wish to begin a collection of theatrical make-up but can only afford a few sticks this is what you might like to start with as they can be your basis for any disguise:—

No: 5	Ivory
No: 6	Sallow Pink
No: 9	Brick Red
No: 16	Deep Brown

With an eyebrow pencil, removing cream and tissues you can now start to experiment.

The secret of removing make-up very easily after you have been disguised is this: **before** you start making up rub a little removing cream all over your face, then wipe it off with a tissue. This will form a barrier on your skin and you will find that the make up not only goes on much more easily, but will wipe off very quickly too when you have finished.

If you play a musical instrument, such as a violin or guitar, use the case to carry pieces of equipment inside.

If you see the chemical formula H_2O written down it simply means ordinary water.

 Sticks of make-up are known as **PAN-STICKS**.

 If you have a map on the wall small flags or coloured pins can be pushed into it to mark positions.

Test your powers of observation with the help of a magazine. Look for a picture of a person and study it. Close the magazine and describe this person to your fellow agent. She or he must then look, through the magazine and see if the person you have just described can be spotted.

Why did the spy scratch himself?

Because nobody else knew where the itch was.

 When you cut faces out of magazines to add to your identikit pictures make sure they are all the same size

 Whatever your disguise make certain that the clothes are comfortable otherwise you will not look right.

The official name for a wren is "Troglodytes".

American secret agents have miniature bugs hidden inside their cuff-links to pick up information at secret dinner parties.

When carrying equipment, clothes with large pockets are much more useful than a lot of bags or packages.

If trailing a suspect in the country **NEVER** have anything hanging around your neck as it could easily get caught on a branch and slow you down.

Carry a small bar of chocolate with you when on a long mission, or a few Barley Sugar sweets, as these will give you energy when you begin to feel tired.

Where would a spy deliver a message in his sleep?

In a pillow-box.

False hair can be stuck safely to your face with a colourless liquid called **SPIRIT GUM**. It is perfectly harmless to use.

Why did the spy tip-toe past the medicine cabinet?

Because he did not want to wake the sleeping pills.

Sticks of theatrical make-up are much cheaper than any liquid or cream make-ups that come in tubes and bottles, and will last for many years.

To reshape your eyebrows cover up your own with a flesh coloured make-up and draw new ones in with an eyebrow pencil.

If you normally wear glasses then by taking them off you can change your appearance quite drastically.

All spies should have a basic knowledge of First Aid in case of emergencies. Find a book at your library or see if your school will hold First Aid classes.

Spy: Doctor, everyone keeps being rude to me!
Doctor: *Get out of here, you silly fool.*

173

 Using some old bandages or strips of material practise on members of your spy ring the art of tying a sling and tying bandages.

 Being watched by the enemy is called being **ILL**.

 Empty cassette cases from tape-cassettes can be used to hide small pieces of equipment in. They can be stored on a cassette rack.

Reconnaissance satellites can transmit pictures of anywhere in the world from 240 km up in space.

All spies should learn to type. Messages and letters can then be typed and there will be no handwriting to give away who has written it.

Computer-controlled Area Sterilisation (CASM) is the term given when thousands of bugging devices are dropped by aircraft.

However brave you are, **NEVER** get involved in a mission that might be dangerous — that is a job for the police.

If on a mission you see something suspicious, such as several days milk on a doorstep that has not been collected, then inform an adult straight away.

 If large areas of your body need to be covered in make-up, you arms for instance, then use a liquid make-up — it saves time and looks much more realistic.

Use pieces of tissue paper to block up any key holes at your headquarters so that nobody can spy through at you.

What do you call a cat that sucks acid drops?

A sour puss.

No living person can speak the ancient language known as **SANSKRIT**.

Keep the furniture in your headquarters highly clean and polished. If anyone leaves any fingerprints they will be visible to the naked eye.

A vanity case makes an excellent box for keeping your disguise make-up in.

 In the country haystacks make very good places to hide behind. You can peep round without being seen if you wear a straw covered hat.

Miniature bugs can be hidden inside large artificial flowers, or even hidden inside real ones.

 Keep an up-to-date address book with all the names and addresses and telephone numbers of friends, family and fellow spies so that you can easily find out where to contact them.

 If a contact coughs three times it means '**there is more than one agent trailing us**'.

If you are pinning maps, instructions or messages on the wall in your hideout, pin them on the same wall as the window, then anyone looking in through the window will not see them.

The human stomach can hold 1.1 litres of liquid.

To make yourself look tired smudge your top eyelid with some red make-up and darken your lower lid with brown or very dark blue. Blend it in carefully.

The insulation in the fuel tanks of rockets is so effective that it would take an ice-cube eight years to melt.

Keep an up-to-date list of postal charges in your hideout. These are available free of charge from any Post Office. If you need to send a letter or parcel quickly you will know how much it will cost.

The Post Office is a good way of saving money. Get your parents to open an account for you and put some money in regularly, even if it is ony 50p a month. It is important that a spy has some savings in case of an emergency.

Keep any old chocolate boxes. Equipment can be hidden inside and they can be placed on your shelves to look like books.

Stick brown paper onto chocolate boxes to give them the appearance of books.

When you are walking on soft ground take a look at the tracks you make. If you are wearing plimsolls or heavy boots you will see how different they look. When next trailing a suspect you will soon be able to tell what kind of shoes he or she is wearing by the tracks.

177

A small suitcase makes an ideal place to keep all your make-up and wigs.

 In the Navy the Semaphore code is widely used.

What is red, runs on wheels, and eats grass?
A bus.
P.S. I lied about the grass.

 If you wish to find out more about the art of disguise visit your local library — there have been many books written on the subject.

 The eyes and mouth are the most expressive parts of your face and so particular care should be taken when making these up.

 Snapping your fingers together is called a **'FILLIP'**.

 The radio was invented by Marconi, who also invented a special secret code to go with it.

 A whistle can be used to send messages in Morse Code.

Special secret marks on the funnels of ships tell us which country the ship comes from.

Test your fellow agents by making a footprint on the ground, or in a tray of wet sand, and get them to guess what kind of shoe you were wearing at the time.

If you are walking only a short distance wear a pair of adults boots. The enemy will see the tracks and look for someone much bigger than yourself.

An old cassette makes a convenient storage place for sticks of theatrical make-up.

Visit art galleries to look at portraits and sculptures to gain ideas for disguise.

The easiest way to apply make-up is to put it on the palm of your hand first, then apply it with your index finger.

An old doorbell can be screwed down to a piece of board and used to send messages in Morse Code.

Knock, knock.
Who's there?
A spy who couldn't reach the doorbell.

The commonest tree in the world is the Larch.

The foot cut from an old stocking provides an excellent cap to wear under a wig as it will keep your own hair perfectly flat.

Tie a bundle of twigs to a piece of string and trail them behind you when walking in the country, that way no footprints will be left.

Test your agents' knowledge of codes by writing out a well-known poem in code and see who is the first to tell you what the poem is.

To make your own code write each letter of the alphabet on a different piece of card. Jumble the 26 cards and lay them out in a row. The first card becomes '**A**', the second '**B**' and so on. Write down the code so that you remember it.

Secret messages in Semaphore can be made clearer by using two different coloured flags — red and green, for example.

A spy poses as a salesman in a sweetshop. He is one metre, sixty-one centimetres tall, and wears size five shoes.
What does he weigh?

Sweets.

Get someone to take a photograph of your face in close-up. It will help you to look at this when you plan any disguise.

A tape-recorder can be invaluable to you when learning how to alter your voice. Play your voice over and over again until it sounds convincing to you.

Record a voice that you hear in the street, or from the radio. Play the recording in secret and attempt to copy the voice and the accent.

Secret messages can be written on the flap of an envelope before you stick it down. The message will then appear on the inside of the envelope.

In Somerset there is a place called Huish Episcopi.

Using a stick of red grease-paint give yourself a larger mouth, it will really alter your appearance.

Our nearest planetary neighbour is Venus, a mere 37 million kilometres away.

If you see something unexpected and suspicious, keep well out of sight and watch carefully without intervening.

A piece of sellotape along the edge of an envelope on any letter you send will make it extra secure and will prevent anyone from steaming the letter open.

Always try and rise very early in the morning so that you can get the mail as soon as the postman delivers it. If there is a confidential letter for you then you will be able to get to it first.

Disguised as a gardener you can work in a greenhouse looking after potted plants. It will be easy for you to see out at all that is happening.

Carry a few sugar cubes with you on any long missions — they will give you energy.

Special messages can be sent to fellow agents by hanging different coloured handkerchiefs on your washing line.

A red handkerchief hanging on a washing line means **DANGER**.

A green handkerchief on a washing line means **'IT'S SAFE TO COME IN'**.

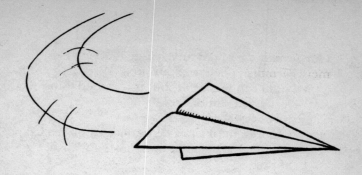

If you are upstairs in your headquarters and
your contact is outside a secret message can be
sent to him concealed in a paper aeroplane.

If you think that someone is guarding your
door then lower any pieces of secret
equipment or secret messages out of the
window on a piece of string to your contact.

When is a red-headed spy like an idiot?

When he's a ginger nut.

In Florida if you see flags flying with red and
black squares in the centre it means that there
is going to be a hurricane.

One of the greatest skills a spy can learn is
how to perform mouth-to-mouth resuscitation,
sometimes called the 'kiss of life'.

If going out on a long mission always tell a
grown up where you are going and when you
expect to return.

Miniature bugs can be hidden in ice cubes, so
look carefully if given a cold drink.

183

Find out about any self-defence courses that are being held in your area. Wrestling and judo can be useful, but it is essential that you get expert guidance.

Rubber masks can be purchased quite cheaply in many joke-shops and make a realistic disguise.

On a hot day the best way to cool down is to have a **hot** drink, such as a cup of tea. You'll find it works.

A good way to start if you decide that you want to become a professional spy is to go to a police cadet training school when you leave school. You might enjoy it so much that you'll prefer to remain in the police force.

Secret documents can be hidden inside the cover of a duvet.

To prevent the key to your hideout getting lost put it on a chain or a piece of string and hang it around your neck.

When on a mission to a very hot country try and remain in the shade as much as possible and use a good sun-tan lotion. A spy cannot afford to be taken ill with sun-stroke.

What do cats strive for?

Purr-fection.

Practise estimating people's ages with your friends, it will help you on missions.

184

Real spies change the colour of their eyes
when in disguise by getting their optician to
them special contact lenses.

If you only have a small map and want a
larger one then take a large piece of paper and
draw the same number of squares on to it,
only larger in size. Then copy each square
accurately from the small map onto the large
piece of paper and you will end up with a big
map.

 Keep a list of all the car numbers of the
vehicles that are regularly parked in your
area. You will then be able to spot when a
strange and unknown car appears.

Try walking with your head down and looking
at the ground. It will make it very difficult for
anyone to see your face.

Empty screw-top jars (such as coffee jars) are
useful for keeping small objects and specimens
in.

Keep talcum powder for fingerprint dusting in
a jar or empty cocoa tin. It will be much
easier to dip your brush in than when using
an ordinary powder shaker.

How did the Vikings send secret messages?

By Norse code.

 Special buzzers, powered by a 4½ volt
battery, can be bought for sending messages
in Norse code.

It is easier to make yourself look fatter than it is to look thinner. The only secret of looking thinner is to lose weight!

Newspaper is full of carbohydrates, and edible **BUT** only in very small quantities.

How do you make a Maltese cross?

Stand on his toe.

 A house or flat is known as a **GAFF**.

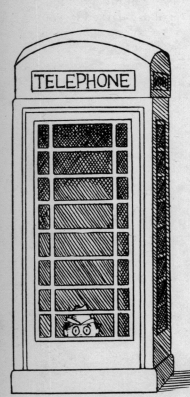

If being chased by an enemy agent try and hide in a telephone box. You can then pretend to be making a call for help and he is sure to disappear.

Label drawers in your headquarters that contain equipment so that you know exactly what is inside.

Wear shorts and you will look like an athelete.

Pretend that you are out jogging and if you spot an enemy you can trail him; if you face danger you can run away to safety.

Ancient Britains disguised themselves when spying by wearing animal skins and painting their bodies with a blue dye.

When sending postcards through the post always put them in an envelope first.

North American Red Indians used feathers and bones as disguises and covered their bodies with ash to make themselves unrecognisable.

A special sign for an agent to enter the room could be when you play a particular tune on the piano or put on a certain record. He can remain hidden until he hears the music as a sign to enter.

What do you call an ape with a gun?

Sir.

In Great Yarmouth, Norfolk, there is a second Nelson's Column. You could fool the enemy by letting them think you were holding a meeting at London's Nelson's Column.

Disguise yourself as a Red Indian by darkening your skin and drawing coloured lines down your cheeks. A headdress can be made from a band of card with feathers stuck on it.

Squirrel is a Greek word meaning '**SHADOW TAIL**'.

An important quality of a spy is to have a lot of enthusiasm, even when you feel really exhausted.

Did you hear about the spy who thought that a Rover 3500 was a bionic dog?

In Iraq you can eat snakes any day of the week except Sunday.

If you have not got time for a proper meal, and you should always make time for a meal wherever you can, then drink a glass of milk. This will give you energy.

Always remember that at the moment you are an amateur spy, so never blunder into a situation that might be dangerous and is a task for an experienced professional spy.

Spies, like detectives, usually cover a specific area which is known as their **PATCH**.

Spies who **always** wear dark glasses usually take a dim view of things!

In hot weather when people wear short-sleeved summer clothes look closely at any tatoos that people have. Tattoos are usually unique and will make that person easily recognisable again.

Garlic is a member of the lily family!

If you are making up to look old remember not only to draw in wrinkles, but remember also that the skin of elderly people is often very sallow and blotchy.

It is essential that a spy is a good swimmer in case of an emergency.

See if there are any life-saving classes at your local baths.

 Keep a complete list of all the equipment in your hideout, then if it is raided you will be able to check what is missing.

 In Indiana, USA, it is illegal to travel on a bus within four hours of eating garlic.

A wide range of false moustaches can be purchased in joke shops, but don't forget when wearing one to change the colour of your eyebrows to match.

Why is a radio never complete?

It is always a wireless.

The human eye can distinguish between two million different colours.

Keep any empty tissue boxes. They provide good storage space for equipment.

Never trespass on any private land, such as farmland, without permission; otherwise you could get yourself into serious trouble.

Any breakable pieces of equipment can be kept inside old socks for protection.

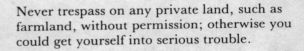

If a contact across a crowded room rubs both eyes at once it means '**KEEP A LOOK OUT**'.

Code names for agents in your spy ring can simply be their initials. David Knight, for example, would be known as 'DK'.

Always read your local newspaper each week. That way you will be kept up to date with all events in your area.

A fun way of testing the ability of your agents to disguise themselves is to hold a Fancy Dress Party and see who can come up with the cleverest and most convincing disguise.

What training would you need to be a rubbish collector?

None, you just pick it up as you go along.

What is as big as an elephant, but doesn't
weigh anything?

An elephant's shadow.

A periscope is a useful piece of equipment that
enables you to see around corners.

When writing letters always keep your hands
washed and clean so that no obvious inky
fingerprints are left on the paper.

If wearing a wig then use extra thick make-up
on your hairline to cover up the join.

Obtain from your library a book of flags from
around the world then if you see a flag on a
ship or on the side of a plane you will know
immediately which country it comes from.

Spy: Doctor, doctor, I keep thinking I'm a
dumpling.
Doctor: *Don't get into such a stew.*

If a good spy story appears at your local
cinema then go along with all the members of
your spy ring so that you can all learn some
useful tips together.

When combing wigs always use a soft brush.
A comb or strong brush will pull the hairs out
and damage the wig.

Always make certain that you know how
much you weigh yourself, then by comparing
someone in size to yourself you will be able to
estimate their approximate weight.

When sticking on a moustache made of crêpe
hair start from just above your top lip and
work upwards towards your nose so that the
hair overlaps correctly.

Always be prepared for disappointments.
Even professional spies are not successful in
their missions all the time.

Secret messages can be passed on at school be
sellotaping them to the bottom of a desk until
they are collected.

A spy test can be performed at your
headquarters. Send one spy out of the room.
The rest pick one spy to be an enemy agent.
The spy sent outside must then come in and
try and discover which the enemy agent is. He
can ask what questions he likes but the spies
can only answer yes or no. Only the 'enemy'
agent is allowed to lie. Having guessed
correctly the one chosen as the enemy leaves
the room next and the operation is repeated.

SPY THOUGHT FOR THE DAY: It's
better to keep your mouth shut and let people
think you are an idiot than open it and prove
them right.

A good hideout and observation post is in the
tower of a castle or church steeple. Pretend
that you are a tourist and then when in the
highest part of the building you can look down
below with your binoculars.

Why did the spy avoid the cemetary?

He wouldn't be seen dead there.

If you stick crêpe hair on to gauze before applying it to your face it can be used over and over again.

Disguised as a postman you can call at the enemy headquarters you can collect any mail that they have to be sent. You can then intercept any secret messages.

Semaphore was used by spies long before any telegraph or telephone had been invented. It was also used on the railways as a method of sending signals.

The sand of Kauai in Hawaii makes a noise like a dog barking when stepped on.

Keep a fake book of names and addresses so that if stolen the enemy will have no idea who your fellow spies or relations are.

What did the bald spy say when he was given a comb?

I'll never part with it.

If an invisible ink calls for a chemical developer then place the paper directly into the developer downwards, and do not move it about otherwise the message will smudge. To read the message lift it straight out.

If a secret message is wet with the developer lay it on a sheet of blotting paper. In this way you will not damage the furniture in any way.

When deciphering messages remember that
'z' is the least common letter of the English
language.

Miniature bugging devices are often attached
magnetically to lampshades hanging from the
centre of a room. These will then pick up a
conversation from any point in the room.

A very quick way of changing your
appearance if you are a female spy is simply to
tie a scarf around your head so that it covers
your hair completely.

The third hand on a watch is in fact the
second hand.

In the English language there are certain
letters that frequently occur together, such as
QU and **TH**, and this should be remembered
when decoding messages.

Here are the top twenty most commonest
groups of two letters that frequently occur
together:

TH	**IN**	**ES**	**OR**	**HE**
AN	**RE**	**ER**	**ON**	**AT**
ND	**ST**	**EN**	**OF**	**TE**
ED	**TI**	**HI**	**AS**	**TO**

Why did the spy put sugar under his pillow?

He wanted sweet dreams.

Never discard old pieces of material, blankets, sheets or curtains, for even though they may seem of little use for a disguise it is amazing what you may need at a later date, and they can always be made up into clothes by someone who can sew.

If an enemy agent attempts to stop and speak to you pretend that you are unable to speak English and make your escape as quickly as you can.

The sounds which carry best and are easiest for the human ear to hear are, "**ah**", "**aw**", "**eh**", "**ee**" and "**oo**".

 When dogs follow a man's trail they follow the scent he leaves in each of his footprints. Even humans can follow a fresh trail if it has been left on a firm floor, and if they are prepared to go down on all fours and sniff!

Spies have to be clear-thinking and smooth-talking. Test yourself with this top-secret tongue-twister: "**Spies spy mince pies.**" Say it five times without making a single mistake!

1000 JOKES: THE GREATEST JOKE BOOK EVER

Gyles Brandreth; illustrated by Nick Berringer
0   552   54159   1   75p

* Teacher: Why do we sometimes call the Middle
         Ages the Dark Ages?
  Betty: Because they had so many knights.

* Did you hear about the vegetarian cannibal?
  He would only eat Swedes.

* Percy: How do fishermen make their nets, Dad?
  Dad: Easily. They just take a lot of holes and sew
         them together.

* 'But Cecil, it isn't our baby.'
  'Shut up — it's a better pram.'

* Maud: Samantha reminds me of a film star.
  Ivy: Really, which one?
  Maud: Lassie.

* Our next comedian is so bad that when he took
  part in an open-air show, twenty-six trees got up
  and walked out.

1000 FASCINATING FACTS: THE GREATEST
BOOK OF AMAZING INFORMATION EVER
KNOWN
Gyles Brandreth; illustrated by Diana Gold

0 552 54165 6   75p

* Richard III, Louis XIV and Napoleon Bonaparte
were all born with teeth.

* In 1970 a Texan swallowed 225 live goldfish.

* Flies take off with a backward jump.

* Wealthy women in seventeenth century Russia
wore pearl-studded hats to hide their heads, which
were shaved at their marriage ceremony.

* The manufacturers of 'Monopoly' print more
'money' than the whole of the United States
Treasury.

* The human mouth produces 2-3 pints of saliva a
day.

1000 RIDDLES: THE GREATEST BOOK OF
RIDDLES EVER KNOWN
Gyles Brandreth; illustrated by Diana Gold

0   552   54166   4   75p

* What is the difference between a doormat and a
    bottle of medicine?

* What is the best exercise for losing weight?

* How do sailors get their clothes clean?

* Why are a star and an old barn alike?

* What is worse than biting into an apple and finding
    a worm?

* What smells most in a chemist shop?

* HOW MANY RIDDLES DO YOU KNOW?

1000 QUESTIONS: THE GREATEST QUIZ BOOK EVER KNOWN
Gyles Brandreth; illustrated by Nick Berringer

0   552   54158   3   65p

* Which is the largest island on Earth?

* Who was the first man to walk in space?

* How many muscles do you use when you frown?

* What type of animal is the 'black widow'?

* Which is larger: a litre or a quart?

* In what industry is a clapper-board used?

* What is the single word used as the international distress call?

* HOW MANY QUESTIONS WERE YOU ABLE TO ANSWER?

THE CRAZY ENCYCLOPAEDIA
Gyles Brandreth; illustrated by Bobbie Craig

0 552 54174 5   75p

AN A-TO-Z OF TOTAL LUNACY!

COMPILED BY CRACKPOTS!

TELLS YOU NOTHING YOU EVER WANTED
TO KNOW!

GUARANTEED USELESS!

NO OTHER ENCYCLOPAEDIA LIKE IT!

ANCIENT JOKES, BRAIN BOGGLERS,
DAFFYNITIONS, IGNORANCE, KNOCK
KNOCKS, NOLEDGE, ODES AND ENDS,
SPORTS, TWERPSICHORE, U.F.O.s, WIT-
CHES AND WIZARDS, and CRAZY X, Y.
Z . . . .

THE CRAZY WORD BOOK
Gyles Brandreth; illustrated by Jacqui Sinclair

0 552 54182 6   75p

From amazing A to zippy Z — this magnificent hotchpotch of word power and fun will take your brain cells by storm!

Dabble with homophones, agonise over anagrams, astound a friend with a nippy palindrome, mix up a mnemonic memory booster, and cross swords with cross words.

Word pictures, word squares, word games, word codes and word quizzes galore — become a wordomaniac with this crazy, crazy, word book.

THE CRAZY BOOK OF WORLD RECORDS
Gyles Brandreth; illustrated by Mike Miller

0 552 54196 6   85p

Are you a record breaker?

CAN YOU —

balance more than seven golf balls on top of each other?

stand on one leg for more than 19 hours?

shell 12 hard-boiled eggs in less than 1 minute 59 seconds?

write a sentence containing over 908 three-lettered words?

slice a 2lb onion into more than 157 slices?

These and many more flabbergasting feats and incredible firsts set down by young people all over the world will amaze, astound and, best of all, challenge YOU to be a world-class, number one record winner, too . . .

THE DAFT DICTIONARY
Gyles Brandreth; illustrated by Ian West

0 552 54128 1   60p

An A-Z of ordinary words with quite extraordinary meanings!

Hundreds of unique daffynitions!!!

D entist: someone who always looks down in the mouth.

A ppear: something you fish off.

F leece: insects that get into your wool if you don't wash properly.

T axidermist: a stuffed cab driver.

H ippies: the things you hang your leggies on.

I llegal: a sick bird of prey.

No other dictionary like it in the world!!!!!

THE BIG BOOK OF MAGIC

Gyles Brandreth; illustrated by Peter Stevenson

0   552   54177   X   80p

Presenting, among a treasury of flabbergasting feats and sleights-of-hand, that mind-boggling, stupendous trick — BOTTLIN' EGGS in which with the aid of 1 egg, some vinegar and a bottle, you proceed to insert the egg through the neck of the bottle WITHOUT BREAKING THE SHELL!

How's it done? That's the secret! And if you don't want egg on your face, careful study of this won-drous volume, crammed with tricks, aids and hints to inspire awe and admiration, will produce . . . magical results!

THE BIG BOOK OF OPTICAL ILLUSIONS
Gyles Brandreth; illusions by Albert Murphy

0 552 54155 9   65p

If you dare to open a copy of this unbelievable book, be prepared for moving specks before your eyes, grey spots that appear and disappear, solid objects that cannot exist, straight lines that wave and bend, gyrating circles, pulsating patterns and mazes that muddle the mind!

DO NOT believe anything you see . . . DO NOT attempt to read this book with a weak stomach . . . YOU HAVE BEEN WARNED . . .

CHALLENGE

Gyles Brandreth; illustrated by Peter Stevenson

0   552   54194   X   85p

Can you eat a bowl of soup with a fork?

Can YOU blow a bubble to beat the world bubble gum record?

Can YOU put on every single pair of socks you own — one after the other?

Can YOU do up your buttons, peel a banana and comb your hair without using your thumbs?

Challenges for journeys, challenges for rainy days, challenges alone and challenges with friends — treasure hunts, brain busters, puzzles, tricks and daredevil dares . . . can you take a CHALLENGE?

If you would like to receive a newsletter telling you about our new children's books, fill in the coupon with your name and address and send it to:

Gillian Osband,

Transworld Publishers Ltd,

Century House,

61–63 Uxbridge Road, Ealing,

London, W5 5SA

_____

Name ....

Address ....

....

CHILDREN'S NEWSLETTER

All the books on the previous pages are available at your bookshop or can be ordered direct from Transworld Publishers Ltd., Cash Sales Dept. P.O. Box 11, Falmouth, Cornwall.

Please send full name and address together with cheque or postal order—no currency, and allow 45p per book to cover postage and packing (plus 20p each for additional copies).